Praise for *The Truth About Love*

"Dr. Pat Love hits an extraordinary home run for all the players in the love relationship. No reader will leave this book the same way he or she began. Within its pages, you will find the humanity, precision, clarity, and direction needed to create a profound and lasting love. As a clinician and trainer of therapists, this important book will be an essential read for all those I encounter. Bravo to Pat Love for this gift to us all."
—Sunny Shulkin, ACSW, master trainer, Imago Relationship
 Therapy and cofounder, Imago Education

"Pat Love delivers an excellent handbook for the married or single person. She tells the 'truth about love' and does so in a way that will improve or perhaps save thousands of relationships. A must read no matter what state your love life is in."
—John Lee, author of *The Flying Boy* and *Growing Yourself Back Up*

"This is the best relationship book I have read. It speaks to all people about how to make our intimate connections satisfying and loving. It is a friendly book that is based on the most up-to-date research. From infatuation to forever, Pat Love highlights the truth about love."
—Jon Carlson, Psy.D., Ed.D., ABPP, past president, International Association of Marriage & Family Counselors and
 cohost, *Living Love* video series

"In this priceless book, Pat Love offers profound insights into the nature and pitfalls of intimacy in long-term relationships. Then she goes on to recommend steps couples can take as they work to recapture the joyful love so many have lost. This book is the answer to love-starved partners' prayers."
—Richard B. Stuart, author of *Helping Couples Change*
 and *Second Marriage*

"The soul searching quizzes and practical advice about compatibility, commitment, and chemistry will empower individuals and couples to nurture and protect their relationships. If people at all stages of a relationship learned the difference between growing to love someone versus falling in love, I would see far fewer people dealing with the trauma of infidelity."
—Shirley P. Glass, Ph.D., ABPP, author of *The Trama of Infidelity: Research and Treatment*

"There are a lot of books about love. What makes this one unique is that it's a loving book about love. With compassion, it takes us by the hand—and by the heart—and guides us home. Pat Love doesn't lecture us about how we have to really care—she knows we care so much that our failures break our hearts. She knows we are committed and we'll do whatever it takes—if someone will simply show us how. Her gentle, accessible stories and illuminating, practical exercises take us—imperfect people—to the promised land. After reading this book, you feel like the little engine that could . . . I think I can, I think I can. You approach the mountain of love with a smile on your face all fired up with confidence."
—Diane Sollee, director, Coalition for Marriage, Family and Couples Education, LLC (CMFCE)

THE Truth ABOUT Love

The Highs, the Lows, and

How You Can Make It Last Forever

Pat Love, Ed.D.

A Fireside Book

Published by Simon & Schuster

NEW YORK • LONDON • TORONTO • SYDNEY • SINGAPORE

FIRESIDE
Rockefeller Center
1230 Avenue of the Americas
New York, NY 10020

FIRESIDE and colophon are registered trademarks
of Simon & Schuster, Inc.

Designed by Elina D. Nudelman

Manufactured in the United States of America

10   9   8   7   6   5   4

Library of Congress Cataloging-in-Publication Data

Love, Patricia.
    The truth about love: the highs, the lows, and how you can make it last forever / Pat Love.
        p.   cm.
    "A Fireside book."
    Includes index.
    1. Marriage.   2. Man-woman relationships.   3. Love.   4. Intimacy (Psychology)
I. Title.

HQ734 .L756 2001
306.81—dc21   Library of Congress Control Number: 2001018975

ISBN 0-684-87188-2

Excerpts on pages 150–51 are reprinted with the permission of Simon & Schuster from
These Are a Few of My Favorite Things by Tony Burton. Copyright © 1999.

This book is dedicated to Spanky and our gang

Contents

THE Truth ABOUT Love

Introduction

My husband was just about to wake me with a cup of coffee when my eyes popped open at four o'clock the morning we left for the Virgin Islands. As I slowly eased myself into a semi-prone position to get the caffeine to my lips, I could hear him singing in the bathroom. Smiling to myself, I reflected on the absurdity of me, the night owl, living with Spanky, the lark. Twenty minutes later, as I shuffled past him shaving at the sink, I couldn't help but chuckle at the dance routine he had added to his vocal performance. His eye caught my amused look in the mirror and he gave me that smile that still creates butterflies in my stomach all these years later. In this fleeting moment of connection, I was filled with appreciation and gratitude to be living in a state of true love—for this has not always been the case.

I can vividly remember when I had little understanding of the true nature of love. The despair of one particular night many years ago still stands out in my mind as if it were yesterday. It began with an all too familiar conversation with my former husband.

"Are you coming to bed?" he asked.

"Umm, a little later," I replied.

Translation: "Do you want to make love?" Answer: "No." The scene was familiar, but this time I felt a hopelessness that set this exchange apart from all the other invitation-and-refusal scenes we'd enacted before. When I finally got to bed the space between us was like a demilitarized zone, bunkered by two cold backs facing opposite directions. The positions were familiar but the numbness was new. It seemed only a night ago that we had gone to sleep in our peacetime position with his arm around me and my head snuggled between his shoulder and neck. That night I knew what I had not accepted before. We would never sleep in that luscious slumber of lovers again. Tired of the conflict, guilt, and inadequacy—and feeling like a failure as a wife and a woman—I gave up hope and collapsed into despair. I couldn't have felt more alone. I knew then that the loneliest night you can ever spend could be lying next to someone you love.

I don't know if you can pinpoint the exact moment when hope goes out of a marriage, but looking back, that night seems like a turning point to me. I had never felt such desperation. Before then, we had always managed to surmount our difficulties and get back to a loving connected place, but after that night, it was never the same. Although it would be years before we would separate, I think the grieving began with this incident. A relationship that started with such high hopes and optimism had slowly turned into a profound disappointment.

To this day I find it hard to accept the way that relationship ended. Anyone looking at our early life together could easily have seen us as the perfect couple. Our courtship was old-fashioned and romantic. We spent long hours walking, talking, and getting to know each other before we even shared a kiss, and we took time to deepen our friendship through sharing experiences like swimming in a nearby stream and taking part in volunteer projects. With the energy between us, we could make even the most mundane activity interesting.

In the early years of matrimony, our excitement—fueled by strong sexual desire and great lovemaking—quickly spread to numerous new adventures afforded by marriage: moving, traveling, visiting relatives, entertaining, making new friends, and later conceiving our first child. Shortly after giving birth, however, I noticed that my sexual desire had dropped out of sight and, frankly, I didn't miss it. I was busy being a full-time mother, plus trying to manage all the responsibilities I'd had prior to the birth. I didn't have time to think about sex. My lack of interest was not a problem for me, but it was clearly—and rightfully—a problem for my husband. At the time, I silently blamed him for being inconsiderate enough to desire me when the feeling wasn't mutual. We got into a pattern of withholding. I withheld sex; he withheld intimacy. I quit sharing my body; he quit sharing his feelings. We both managed our fears and loneliness by repressing our needs and staying very busy. Sadly, over the course of time I began to believe that we were trapped in an unbearably incompatible marriage that doomed one of us to everlasting sexual frustration and the other to rejection and withdrawal. These convictions led to an action that remains the deepest regret of my life: an unnecessary divorce from a thoroughly decent, loving man and the father of my two children. We believed we had fallen out of love. Now I know that we had simply entered a different stage of love.

Psychological pain can paralyze or motivate you. For years I was emotionally frozen over the sorrow and remorse surrounding my divorce, but over time I became driven by the need to understand how it happened and then to prevent it from happening again to myself, as well as others. First, I enrolled in a doctoral program and began studying marriage and family therapy. After receiving my degree, I accepted a graduate faculty position where I could continue to focus my attention like a laser beam on the subject of love relationships. I also began working with couples through workshops, couples therapy, and lectures. I became an outstanding example of "you teach what you need to know." Over the past twenty years I have continued my study and gathered a wealth of information from research, colleagues, clients, and my own life experience. This book is a culmination of the knowledge that has now helped thousands of people—including me—understand the truth about love and create a love that can last forever. I am delighted to be sharing it with you.

To begin our journey toward understanding the true nature of love, let's take a closer look at marriage, because during much of the twentieth century, love and marriage were inexorably linked. When two people fell in love, they got married and settled down. Matrimony was a rite of passage into adulthood and nearly everyone took that route. Today, that is not always the case. In 1999, the Rutgers University National Marriage Project reported marriage to be at a forty-year low, with more and more people not only delaying marriage, but not choosing it at all. The main reason people give is fear that "they won't be satisfied." Sadly, research bears this out. The percentage of people who reported being "very happy" in their marriages fell from 53.5 percent in the years from 1973 to 1976 to 37.8 percent in 1996. This is such a cause for concern that the federal and state governments are enacting marriage covenant laws and urging Congress to eliminate marriage penalties in the tax codes. In addition, some high schools are beginning to add marriage education skills to the curriculum, which is a long overdue effort.

There are many reasons that the structure and quality of marriage is being called into question today more than any other time in our history. Only a few decades ago the model of marriage was quite simple. The woman was the homemaker and the man earned the wages. The goal of marriage was to establish a home, have children, and get ahead economically. Success was easily determined. Today, this *Happy Days* model of marriage comprises the minority of U.S. families. During the past fifty years traditional marriage has been affected by free love in the 1960s, open marriage in the 1970s, the acceptance of cohabitation in the 1980s, and finally a 50 percent divorce rate in the 1990s.

Families now come in a wide variety of models, and most would agree that matrimony has gotten more complex. This is both good news and bad news. Today, there are a lot more entrées on the marriage menu, but it's a tall order. We now expect friendship, support, fun, intimacy, and good sex—not to mention personal growth and life fulfillment. The job description for a long-term partner might include cook, housekeeper, dry cleaner, masseuse, therapist, best friend, sex surrogate, nurse, mind reader, coach, mechanic, carpenter, lawn specialist, entertainer, social secretary, chauffeur, accountant, automatic teller, and loan officer. Unfortunately, a marriage license doesn't come with a job description or a set of instructions. There is definitely "some assembly required." In fact, putting together a modern-day marriage can be likened to assembling an airplane in flight.

It is clear that while the number of options for relationships has gone up, the satisfaction level has gone down. Despite this fact, there is evidence that marriage is still highly valued. The vast majority of us still marry and remarry in spite of the terrible odds. "Having a satisfying love relationship" is cited as the number one goal of mature adults ahead of wealth, health, and satisfying work. There is good reason. University of Chicago researcher Dr. Linda Waite discovered what she calls "the marriage mortality benefit." Statistics show that married men and women live longer. They also drink less alcohol, use fewer drugs, and have more money. A good marriage can help protect people from illness and disease, and it can help them bounce back more quickly if they do get sick. A divorced man is twice as likely to die in any given year from heart disease, stroke, hypertension, or cancer. Death for the divorced is four times more likely via automobile accidents and suicide, seven times higher by cirrhosis of the liver and pneumonia, and eightfold greater by murder. Single women are two to three times as likely to die of all forms of cancer. No wonder we continue to tie the knot even though the divorce rates give us a 50-50 chance that it won't stay tied.

But in order to gain the numerous benefits marriage or any relationship can offer, you have to know the truth about love. The evidence is clear that without proper information and guidance, you can easily make serious mistakes. For example, you might make the same mistake I did and confuse a normal stage of love with the end of love. When my sexual desire for my husband changed and started to wane, I believed I was falling out of love. I now know the change in my libido was normal. Most women will feel little sexual desire right after the birth of a baby. This is nature's way of focusing your attention on caring for the infant instead of conceiving another child. But because I believed sexual attraction and love were synonymous—which is not true—I thought there was something seriously wrong with the relationship. Once I started to believe this, I began to look for other problems and, of course, I found them.

When you hold a negative belief and have no facts to offset this perception, subsequent thoughts tend to follow that point of view. This is called confirmation bias, meaning we have the tendency to pay more attention to information consistent with our beliefs. If you believe your relationship is in trouble, you will be looking for all the signs to validate that position. Once the seed of doubt has been planted, you may find yourself gathering evidence to support your case. When the majority of your thoughts are negative, you don't feel like you are in love. Most of the serious problems in relationships stem from the fact that people do not understand the true nature of love. Misconceptions can lead to destructive conclusions. For example, many of us have been led erroneously to believe that happy, stable couples:

- Never argue.
- Are not dependent on one another.
- Both want sex equally.
- Never get angry.
- Get all their needs met.
- Share responsibilities equally.
- Never feel lonely.

- Always agree.
- Think alike.
- Never get bored.
- Always know what the other wants.
- Resolve all their problems.

None of these statements is true.

Today, thanks to research, we know more about the true nature of love and satisfying relationships than ever before. The last five years have given us more sound information than any other time in our history. We now have a high degree of certainty about what makes marriages work—and what doesn't work. We know that love doesn't last; you have to *make* it last. We also know that love goes through predictable cycles and that each has unique characteristics and purpose. Understanding the true nature of love is the key to happiness in relationships.

Most of us do not have an accurate picture of what a true love looks like. I don't know about you, but I came into adulthood without a clear vision of a healthy love relationship. My parents divorced when I was in first grade, my grandparents were divorced years before that, and the family members who had loving relationships lived too far away to visit. Without examples of true love at close hand, my models of love had to come from songs, books, friends, movies, and television. Isn't that a scary thought! Just take a look at this list of "love stories" from our culture and what they teach us about relationships:

Romeo and Juliet

Casablanca

Dr. Zhivago

The English Patient

Bridges of Madison County

Titanic

If you credit the models set forth in these screen examples, you believe that true love will be short, intense, forbidden, and unrequited. In order to stay in love, you must die or never live together! Furthermore, every one of these relationships is limited to the very earliest stage of love—infatuation. We know that true love requires basically three elements: chemistry, compatibility, and commitment. The lovers in these stories certainly had chemistry, but they never stayed together long enough to determine whether they were compatible or committed. They barely got to first base.

A couple years ago HBO was premiering *Bridges of Madison County* and touting it as "the love story of the century." The first time I heard that ad I thought to myself: "This is great job security. As long as our society believes that *Bridges of Madison County* is the love story of the century, I will have a job!" If a brief, clandestine encounter is equated with true love, no wonder marriage is in trouble. It's easy to spend three days with someone and then pine away without further contact. We did that in adolescence. How hard can it be?

One could argue that there are movies about couples who live happily ever after—like *When Harry Met Sally* or *Runaway Bride*—but they never show you how they did it! We get to see two people go through an hour and thirty-seven minutes of misunderstanding and frustration, then go romantically off into the sunset. We never get to see what happens next. This is not to say the motion picture industry is entirely to blame. Movie moguls are simply responding to a public that seems largely interested in falling in love, not staying in love. However, this limited perception of love and marriage has led us to serious misconceptions, such as:

- Infatuation equals love.
- If it isn't perfect, it wasn't meant to be.
- Once love dies, you can never get it back.
- Chemistry is all that matters.
- There is one true soul mate for everyone.
- Love conquers all.
- If a relationship is tough, it means you have the wrong partner.
- You can't rekindle passion.
- If you are really in love, you won't be attracted to other people.
- If you meet the right person, you will live happily ever after.

These and other delusions have contributed to the inflated sense of discouragement many couples feel when their relationship hits a normal and predictable challenge. They can also lead individuals to give up perfectly good relationships only to find that the same difficulties show up the next time around. Until we understand the nature of love, we are destined to live in a state of disappointment. This book can prevent that from happening. In fact, no matter how long you have been together or how unrewarding your relationship may be, at any point you can change it for the better. One person can transform a relationship. If you change your behavior, the relationship cannot stay the same. Another common misconception about love is that it is a static state: once you fall in love, you get on a high and stay there forever. This is not true. The course of true love consists of a series of highs and lows. You can gain comfort not only in knowing that the peaks and valleys are inherent to love, but that they are shared by millions of people around the world. You are never alone in your relationship.

Understanding this was enough to help one young couple I worked with. Heather called me frantically trying to get into an upcoming couples seminar I had scheduled. The workshop was already full to capacity, so I suggested they come to the next one. "We have to come to this one," the woman pleaded. "We are supposed to get married in two weeks, and right now the wedding is canceled. Please, please let us come. We'll sit on the floor if we have to."

Hearing that, I couldn't refuse.

The morning of the workshop they arrived and took a place in the group of couples ranging from their own age to the age of their grandparents. Throughout the two days Heather and her fiancé, Jason, sat quietly and hardly said a word, but it was clear they were taking in the information. At the end of the weekend, they got up and told the story of canceling their wedding and begging to get into the workshop. Then they proudly announced that the wedding was back on. The whole workshop burst into applause. I was feeling quite proud and a little curious about what particular skill or experience had given them the confidence to proceed. The bride-to-be answered my question. "After sitting here for two days and listening to everyone's problems, we realize that our problems are just like everyone else's. If you all can make it, so can we."

This young couple came to the workshop with a lot to learn about the nature of true love, and they needed a frame of reference that included an understanding of their highs and lows as a natural, normal part of the continuing story of every relationship. Once they attained this perspective and saw that their experience was no different than that of fifty other couples, they were able to relax and comfortably move into the commitment of marriage and begin their journey toward enduring love.

Another common misconception related to love is that it is one-dimensional, or that it takes only one form. Most people tend to equate love with the behaviors and feelings common to the initial stage of infatuation, when, in reality, this is just the beginning of love. The purpose of this book is to guide you through all the stages of love, from infatuation to the deep connection that is the hallmark and destination of true love.

If you are reading this and wondering if the relationship you have now could possibly qualify for the love I describe, the answer is yes. The final misconception is that love is a feeling and you either have it, or you don't. The fact is that love grows in response to getting your needs met, and there are specific, proven strategies that can help you create the love you long for. This book is a step-by-step guide for developing each skill you will need to set forth on your own path to true love with the partner you already have.

I consider it part of my mission in life to set the record straight concerning love. A large part of the passion I carry for this subject has come from mistakes I've made in the past, as well as the heartache I have seen in the lives of my clients and friends. I am convinced that much of the distress I've observed, as well as experienced, could have been prevented had the truth been known about love.

This book is my attempt to pass on to you the information that can help us all live happier lives. My vision is twofold: first, to describe the nature of love, which will enable you to navigate the highs and lows plus gain the lessons each of love's stages has to offer; and second, to serve as a guide for creating relationship strategies that will lead to long-term happiness. The book is directed toward those of you who are in a committed relationship and desire to make it more satisfying. It is also written for those of you who are just starting a relationship, or are trying to gain an understanding of the phenomenon of love before you find a partner. If I had had the information contained in this book, it could have changed the course of my life. My fondest hope is that it will do that for you. I hope that soon you will be living your life intimately connected to a loving partner with a love far deeper than infatuation; enjoying the pleasure of mutually gratified needs; fulfilling one another's expectations of love; and reaping all the benefits of true love.

1

Infatuation: The First Stage of Love

FALLING IN LOVE

The first time Lauren laid eyes on Keith it was clear the rumor mill had not exaggerated his good looks. Looking at him across the workout room, there was no mistake that this hunk with the towering frame and chiseled face was the guy her girlfriends had been talking about. Determined not to be distracted, Lauren cranked up the difficulty on her spin cycle and tried to focus on her technique, but her eyes kept wandering in his direction. One time he caught her looking at him and, embarrassed, she went on with her workout and made sure she didn't glance his way again. Two days later he was the first person she ran into when she walked into the gym. Keith spoke first, and Lauren made a brief response as she continued toward the women's locker room. Throughout her workout that day, she made a point not to look for him, but she held in her stomach just in case he might be watching.

During the next few days, she was too busy to visit the gym but found herself wondering if he was there. When she went back the following week, she was pleased to see him and loved it when he made special notice of her. "Hey, I haven't seen you in a couple days. You been out of town?" he called from the bench press.

"No, just busy," Lauren replied, wishing she had sounded more friendly. Another chance came later when he walked over to talk as she was finishing her leg lifts. This time they had a pleasant conversation, and she was pleased to find he was much more down-to-earth than his good looks might lead one to believe. Over the next few weeks, chatting became a regular part of their workout regimen, and each time they talked there was more energy between them. Lauren was very attracted to Keith, and she spent a good deal of time fantasizing that he felt the same. Finally, one evening he asked her to go out for coffee after their workout. During the course of their private conversation, she began to think he did have feelings for her and felt delighted when he asked her out for the weekend. A month and several dates later, Lauren's feelings for Keith had grown enormously, and she decided to share this information with her two closest friends. When she told them, they were not surprised. In fact, they had suspected it—first by her lack of time and attention to them, and second, by the way she couldn't stop smiling at the mention of his name. Lauren admitted she had never felt happier and silently believed she'd met the man of her dreams.

There is no experience more magical than falling in love. Coming under the spell of infatuation is considered by many to be the apex of life, and has inspired authors and artists from every culture throughout time. Poetry, prose, lyrics, sculpture, drawings, architecture, war, ceremony, life, and death have honored love. It is an experience humans never seem to tire of and also one that can occur when you least expect it. People have been known to fall in love during an argument, riding on an airplane, serving on jury duty, conversing via e-mail, and probably during most life events. One of my former clients met her husband at a funeral—further illustrating that love is indiscriminant of circumstances. Think back to the last time you fell in love. You felt magnetized and full of luscious energy. Just the sight of the person could zap your body with a thousand-watt current that transformed you from a reasonably rational, functional adult into a trembling puddle of pure yearning. Your feelings went beyond words. You could get lost in your lover's eyes and get high on that special scent of aftershave or cologne. Being together transformed the most mundane activity—such as going to Wal-Mart for a pair of scissors—into a deeply rewarding occasion.

As unique as it feels to you when you're in it, infatuation is universal. Lovers around the world report similar feelings and behaviors. But until recently, we had little insight into this ubiquitous phenomenon. Now research has given us a wealth of new information that demystifies infatuation and reveals the truth about love. Let's take a field trip into neurobiology and find out what's going on when we enter this magical world.

IT'S NOT (INITIALLY) ABOUT SEX

From the outset it is important to distinguish infatuation from sex drive, which is simply the craving for sexual gratification. Humans can feel the urge for sex with someone without having romantic inclinations. When you are aroused, any number of partners can give you simple sexual relief. Infatuation is different. You can be attracted to a number of people but infatuated with only one at a time. Infatuation is characterized by focused attention on a specific partner. When you are infatuated with someone, only this person can give you those euphoric "in love" feelings. When you encounter a candidate, the first sign is likely to be heightened interest—sometimes in the form of irritation or annoyance—but more often with the innocent enjoyment of one another's company. "Love at first sight" can happen, but most often infatuation begins with fondness or comfort in each other's presence. Later there comes a flush or a quickened heartbeat upon encounter, or maybe heightened energy when you are together. As the infatuation continues, separation from your lover creates a great deal of anxiety. When not together, you daydream about reunion and anxiously anticipate the next encounter. To comfort yourself, you might replay former encounters in your mind, sleep with a shirt left behind, listen to a song that reminds you of him or her, or listen to an old message on your answering machine. As the relationship takes on special meaning, you long for further contact and spend time and energy scheming about ways to get together.

In the beloved's presence, you might be uncharacteristically shy or awkward and have difficulty forming coherent sentences. Anxiety and excitement may cause your palms to sweat, your heart to beat faster, and your stomach to feel like the route of a butterfly migration. (Most of us who have spent any time in infatuation's clutches remember the agony, as well as the ecstasy, of this state.) Much of the anxiety comes from your uncertainty about the other person's feelings. For this reason, in the beginning of infatuation, you are highly alert to any statement or act that can be interpreted as favorable. You fantasize and long for signs that your loved one feels the same as you. Once you have confirmation of mutual interest, infatuation takes a quantum leap forward.

When the lover's affection is confirmed, daily priorities get reordered. The workaholic misses deadlines. The penny-pincher blows a paycheck on plane fare. Sleep is sacrificed for intimate encounters. Long phone conversations and/or e-mails abound. Both people have a remarkable ability to emphasize what is admirable in the other partner. They may even feel compassion for negative traits to the extent of turning them into positives ("He is so honest, he told me all about his affairs").

The brain is an incredible creation; it begins working long before your birth and doesn't stop until you fall in love.

The infatuation syndrome is truly an example of Mother Nature at her finest. All the predictable behaviors that accompany the falling-in-love experience are brought on by a naturally orchestrated, drastic change in brain chemistry. When you meet a strong candidate for love, your limbic system is flooded with a powerful chemical concoction—so powerful that scientists now believe that the euphoria of infatuation is a bona fide, altered state of consciousness. It is induced by the action of phenylethylamine (PEA), which is a naturally occurring, amphetamine-like neurotransmitter. Michael Liebowitz, a research psychiatrist at the New York State Psychiatric Institute, explains that when we come into contact with a person who highly attracts us, our brain becomes saturated with a love cocktail comprised of PEA and several other excitatory neurotransmitters, including dopamine and norepinephrine. PEA, known as the "love molecule," works in concert with dopamine and norepinephrine and triggers incredible side effects. Symptoms include a delightfully positive attitude, increased energy, decreased need for sleep, and loss of appetite. Increased concentrations of dopamine in the brain are associated with euphoria. Norepinephrine, which is chemically derived from dopamine, is generally associated with exhilaration, excessive energy, and other excitatory responses.

Sound familiar? It's clear that what we call being in love could also be called being under the influence. Nevertheless, there is a reason for the extreme measures Mother Nature uses to bring us together for this thing called love. It takes a strong chemical force to overpower the amygdala—the brain's inhibition center—which at this point may be trying to warn you, "This isn't smart; you could get hurt!" But the amygdala is no match for this hormonal hurricane. Full-blown infatuation knows no fear. Researchers propose that in the presence of a sufficiently intense attraction, virtually everyone's neural lattices become marinated in natural amphetamines. The frenzied action of lovers' neurons renders them fearless and unrealistically optimistic. It is no wonder that they tend to discount alarming qualities in their sweethearts. You may gently remind a love-struck friend: "Have you really considered the fact that he/she is a practicing alcoholic, has lost three jobs in a row, and has been divorced only two months?" Your friend sweetly responds: "We can work it out." Even in the face of dire information—like "Weren't you alarmed when he got belligerent with that police officer?"—the answer comes back: "He's not that way with me." Adversity just intensifies the influence of the love drugs because PEA is activated, as well as enhanced, by danger, fear, and risk.

When there is uncertainty—in a relationship or any new situation—our awareness is heightened as we seek to determine whether it is safe. In an insecure environment, the body goes to work preparing for fight or flight. The heartbeat increases, awareness is sharpened, blood starts to rush to the face, and palms get sweaty. Once your heart rate reaches 95 beats per minute, adrenaline is dumped into your system, giving you extra energy and putting you in an excited state. Once you have most of the new information, you calm down. When you have a new love interest, sheer novelty accounts for much of the excitement.

PEA, dopamine, and norepinephrine pack such a powerful chemical wallop that people in the throes of infatuation undergo a temporary personality change. A dedicated bookworm might find herself exploring the great outdoors. A devotee of classical music might be found in the front row of a Spice Girls concert. Someone naturally quiet and withdrawn falls in love and can't stop talking. This is why lovers say things like "I can't believe I'm talking to you like this. I'm telling you things I've never told anyone." Or, "You're so easy to talk to." Under the influence of nature's love potion, nontouchers touch, nontalkers talk, and everybody feels happy, and we haven't even gotten to the erotic part yet.

ENTER SEX

We don't need a slew of studies to convince us that sexual energy runs high in the infatuated state, but neurologists report that the sexual euphoria accompanying infatuation is a direct result of the love cocktail. PEA stimulates libido, raising interest in sex. Dopamine makes us more sexually receptive by increasing our enjoyment of sex and making us want it again. Norepinephrine, which is largely responsible for that "swept away" feeling of infatuation, acts like a shot of sexual speed as it hurls us into action. This one-two-three punch from the love potion explains why many times lovers go along for a while claiming "We're just friends" and then wham! They fall into the sexual abyss.

The delightful influence of infatuation makes us dangerously inclined to make decisions we may later regret. When a lover is lavishing time and attention on you, when you wake up in the morning bright-eyed, bushy-tailed, and full of sexual energy, it's easy to believe you have found your long-lost soul mate and will live happily ever after. It is important, though, to realize that infatuation is merely the earliest stage of love. Do not mistake this temporary power surge for a permanent condition, or confuse it with true love.

IT'S ABOUT BIOLOGY

Infatuation is nature's way of getting you to meet, mate, procreate, and produce healthy offspring. In order for this to happen, you must select a partner whose genetic code is compatible with yours. Through early research on tissue rejection in organ transplants, scientists discovered that the body can actually recognize familiar and unfamiliar DNA; in other words, the body has the ability to detect compatible, as well as incompatible, genes. Ursula Goodenough, a researcher at Washington University in St. Louis, found that human genes—specifically those that control the immune system—actually push us toward choosing mates with a different genetic structure. This accounts for the fact that most of us feel no sexual pull toward a brother or sister. Here's how it works.

There is a segment of DNA called the human lymphocyte antigen (HLA), which functions as the immune system's disease detector. An individual's HLA codes for a limited number of diseases and passes on this ability to potential offspring through DNA. However, if this individual mates with a person with a different HLA code, then their offspring will have immunity to far more diseases. This discovery revealed the great evolutionary advantage of mating between a man and woman with dissimilar DNA codes. Consequently, when you come into contact with a suitable DNA match, you will feel an attraction or what we call chemistry. (It's interesting that this term has been around for a long time, but only recently have we come to know just how accurate it is.) This attraction is simply a physiological response to meeting a genetic match. The brain is sending us a signal to move closer and get acquainted.

A T-SHIRT CONTEST FOR MEN!

Claus Wedekind, a noted Swiss researcher, furthered our knowledge about biological attraction when he became curious whether DNA differences in man's secretions affected a woman's attraction to him. To investigate, he designed a very practical experiment. His team recruited one hundred males and females to participate in what is known as the sweaty T-shirt study. The men were given untreated cotton T-shirts to sleep in for two consecutive nights during which time they were not to eat spicy foods, drink alcohol, smoke, or have sex. During the day the T-shirts were kept in a sealed container and after the second night were transported to Wedekind's laboratory. While alone in a room, each woman was asked to rate each man's shirt in terms of sexiness, pleasantness, and aversion. (The study was done around the time the women were ovulating so their sense of smell was most acute.) The study showed that the women rated a man's body odor sexiest and most pleasant when his HLA profiles varied the most from their own. In other words, a woman was most attracted to the scent of the men whose DNA was least like hers. This shows that it's very predictable whom you will find attractive and whom you will not, and that you can have "chemistry" with more than one person.

This may be disappointing, but the fact remains: the initial physical attraction between two people has more to do with biology than love. Attraction evolved to enable individuals to focus their mating effort on preferred partners. When you meet a DNA match, the pleasure centers in the brain are alerted, and the neurotransmitters do the rest. This attraction process, which we have elevated to mystical proportions, is really Mother Nature having her way with you.

Unfortunately, genetic compatibility does not always equal relationship compatibility. More to the point: you can be highly attracted to a jerk! Just because you have chemistry with someone doesn't mean he/she will make a good mate. To determine this, you have to move beyond this early stage. Although there are numerous individuals who qualify as a genetic match, not all would be a compatible mate. The chemistry of infatuation also explains why you can be happily married and/or in love with your current partner and still be attracted to another person. If you meet enough people you will find more than one strong DNA match. I am reminded of one of my favorite movie scenes about infatuation and chemistry. It comes from *Living Out Loud* with Holly Hunter. While looking for the ladies' room in a restaurant, Holly's character inadvertently enters the wrong door and finds herself in the arms of a perfect stranger who, mistaking her for his mistress, grabs her and kisses her passionately. Though initially startled and taken aback, she readily succumbs to this erotic interlude. After an exchange of no more than three minutes, they agree to meet "same time, same place" next week. The following day at work, her smitten look and rosy glow are a dead giveaway to her nursing care patient, who asks why she looks so happy. In vivid detail, she begins to describe this new guy—his attributes, his character, and their future together. When her patient has the audacity to ask his name, she can't answer. And, of course, he doesn't show up the following week for her to find out.

Look at what Webster says about infatuation:

In-fat-u-at-ed 1. Lacking sound judgment; foolish.
2. completely carried away by foolish or shallow love or affection.
3. extrapolating from insufficient information.

The Holly Hunter episode is a great example of Webster's third definition of infatuation—"extrapolating from insufficient information." It's helpful to realize that we can all be attracted to more than one person; that's a biological fact. How we handle the attraction is a statement about who we are and what is important to us.

SELECTIVE MEMORY

From time to time I have had individuals say to me, "Well, I'm not sure I was ever really attracted to my partner." It's been my experience that most often this belief is the result of selective memory. In other words, the person's current feelings or attitudes are coloring his/her perception of the past. When you are bored with your relationship, it's difficult to remember when you were excited. If your relationship is in a slump, it's tough to imagine it otherwise. It is rare that two people get together without initial attraction. When people think that's the case, they usually have just forgotten.

Cheryl Rollins was a good example of a person with selective memory. She and her husband, Alan, came to me for help after being married for nine years. They were discouraged about their relationship and both were feeling lonely and unappreciated by the other. Exhausted from long hours of work and the demands of two young children, they were stretched to the limit. Their time together consisted of taking care of children, doing chores, and watching television. In an attempt to bridge the distance between them and shift the focus in a more positive direction, I asked them: "What was it that attracted you to each other in the first place?" My question was followed by dead silence and blank stares. After a long pause, Cheryl spoke first.

"You know, I've often wondered if we really were attracted to one another or if we were just lonely."

This response got an immediate retort from Alan. "Cheryl, I don't know how you can say that. We were very attracted to each other."

"We were?" Cheryl inquired, her face looking brighter.

"What about all those love letters you wrote me? The cards you sent?" Alan came back, his voice raised, and a smile beginning to appear.

Cheryl said nothing and just looked at him in surprise. After a moment of silence I asked, "Alan, do you still have any of those cards or letters?"

"I think I have all of them."

Cheryl's eyes widened. "You do? Where?"

"They're in the bottom drawer of my desk."

"I had no idea that you had those." Cheryl's face softened.

"I do have them and I can tell you what you said in a lot of them." Alan glanced down at his hands in his lap, then back at Cheryl, whose eyes had begun to moisten. They sat in silence, looking at one another. I had the feeling they were seeing each other for the first time in quite a while.

When these intimate moments happen in a session, I just sit back and silently bathe in the magic. I know the tenderness is very healing for the relationship. After a period of time their gaze was broken with a loving smile, and then they looked at me for direction.

"I'm going to suggest that tonight—after the children are in bed—you get out those letters and read them together. While you are reading, I want you to recapture those early feelings. Recall that period of time in vivid detail—what you did, how you felt, what you loved and enjoyed about each other. Use this experience as a way of continuing the loving energy that began between you here today."

Cheryl and Alan, caught up in the rigors of two jobs, two children—too much—hit a low spot because they were neglecting their relationship. Going back and recalling the earliest stage of love not only helped them recapture wonderful feelings, but it also reminded them of the activities they enjoyed. After a few weeks of reinstating some of these, their marriage was back on course.

NOTABLE EXCEPTIONS

You shouldn't worry if you and your partner didn't experience much intensity in the Infatuation Stage. Many satisfied couples report that they began as friends, then later added a sexual component to their relationship. If this was the case for you, it might even bode well for your future happiness. Ted Huston, Ph.D., a professor at the University of Texas at Austin, found that marriages that begin with romantic bliss and high intensity are particularly divorce-prone because such intensity is too hard to maintain. (I would add that this unhappiness could be due to the unrealistic expectation that this blissful state is supposed to last forever.) Huston further notes that happier couples don't consider the end of infatuation a crushing blow but rather a natural transition from the "romantic relationship" to a "working partnership." He also found that many marriages considered to be lackluster by an observer are not prone to divorce because there is no erosion of the Western-style romantic ideal. It's important to remember that, regardless of how you experienced it, infatuation is distinctly different from true love. First of all, we have so few expectations at the onset of a relationship that any loving gesture is seen as an act of generosity. Plus, every action is greatly influenced by the positive side effects of the chemical high. As stated earlier, even negatives are experienced as positive under the influence of Mother Nature's love potion. If the two of you have a flat tire when you are infatuated, it's an adventure. If the same thing happens when infatuation has waned, it's nothing but a darn nuisance.

TAKING A WORLDVIEW

William Jankowiak of the University of Nevada–Las Vegas and Edward Fischer of Tulane University found evidence of infatuation in 166 cultures they studied. But they also found, in many of these cultures, infatuation did not go hand in hand with matrimony. Instead, it was viewed simply as a force to be dealt with. When you look at societies with the least stable marriages and highest divorce rates, they are the ones that use infatuation as the sole or major criterion for marriage.

Cultures that have broadened their concept of love and utilize outside objectivity in mate selection have much higher marital stability. While I am not suggesting that we turn this most important decision over to parents or another outside source, I do propose that it is time to recognize the scientific facts about love and take a more comprehensive approach to decisions related to it. Throughout my twenty years of clinical practice, I have seen numerous adults make life decisions based upon the euphoria of infatuation only to find disappointment and heartache at the end of the road. There have been families torn apart, perfectly good marriages abandoned, friendships thrown to the wayside, and careers destroyed—all for the brief excitement of an altered state of consciousness. Once the fog lifts and the high wears off—and it will over time—the aftermath of remorse and destruction can be devastating.

WHAT CAN BE LEARNED FROM THE INFATUATION STAGE?

While much of this chapter has been addressing the liabilities of infatuation as a predictor of happiness, it is just as important to investigate what we can learn from this period. The earliest stage of love holds valuable lessons for the couple who aspire to long-term happiness. Infatuation not only serves to get two biologically suited people together; it also provides the prototype for creating lifelong love. Look at what couples do in those first few months:

- They make the relationship a priority.
- They make one another's needs a priority.
- They give one another time and attention.
- They touch one another affectionately.
- They talk of their future together in positive terms.
- They flirt with each other.
- They express their sexual energy.
- They show appreciation.
- They laugh.
- They play.
- They support each other.
- They work out difficulties amicably.
- They overcome great obstacles by working as a team.
- They show love numerous times a day.
- They accept differences.
- They give one another the benefit of the doubt.
- They use energy from the relationship to support work and other personal endeavors.

It's not just the PEA high that makes the Infatuation Stage so delightful. It's also these loving behaviors. Looking at the list, what's not to love? During the Infatuation Stage, nature makes loving easy by reinforcing contact with euphoria-producing neurotransmitters. But she only provides the initial spark. To keep the fires burning, you have to fan the flames. The euphoria of infatuation only lasts about six months and then it slowly begins to wane. By the second year, scientists tell us that lovers are on their own without the aid of Mother Nature's love potion. But you can keep love alive by continuing the loving behaviors. True love is not just a strong feeling. It is an ongoing decision to act in a loving way. Right now, today, begin reinstating some early romantic behaviors. Your relationship will immediately become more satisfying. Loving begets love. This is vital to remember as we leave the Infatuation Stage and venture onto the Post-Rapture Stage of love.

Post-Rapture: The Second Stage of Love

WHEN INFATUATION ENDS, TRUE LOVE BEGINS

If you are reading this book, chances are you have spent some time in the Post-Rapture Stage of love. You might even be experiencing a lull in your relationship right now. If this is true, I say welcome to the club and have no fear. This means you are simply a little further along in the course of true love. Leaving the illusions of infatuation is a necessary step on your journey, and I want to assure you that this temporary low spot is just one of many transitions you will experience as you travel the highways of the heart.

For some people, the end of the Infatuation Stage comes suddenly with a major disagreement or lovers' quarrel, but for most the transition from rapture to real love is gradual. It is marked by subtle changes over time, such as in these examples:

- For months your desires were identical, but lately you don't always want the same things.

- Little habits that once were endearing start to annoy you.

- The social butterfly who used to cancel all his plans to be with you suddenly can't schedule you in every night.

- In recent months there haven't been as many loving gestures between you. You can't remember the last time one of you brought flowers or left a love note.

- Once you were willing to give limitlessly. Now you don't always want to give because you feel like you're not getting as much in return.

- You used to get up early and have your morning coffee together. Now he wants to sleep until the last possible minute and grab a coffee on the way to work.

- You have the feeling that your partner is moving away from you.

- There is more silence between you, whereas before, conversation was effortless.

- You don't have sex as often, and when you do, it takes longer to become aroused and isn't all fireworks every time.

- You feel a need for space and more private time.

- You start seeing things in your partner that you previously overlooked. He's self-absorbed. She's compulsive about housekeeping.

- And most sinister of all: you no longer give the benefit of the doubt; instead, you jump to negative conclusions. He's thirty minutes late: "He's inconsiderate." She requests private time to talk about the relationship: "She's controlling."

The closing of the Infatuation Stage can be marked by behaviors ranging from quiet acceptance to questioning the relationship. Couples whose relationship did not begin with high drama may move past infatuation to the Post-Rapture Stage without fanfare. But other couples who expected the chemical high to last—who equated love with that intense infatuated feeling—may begin to think they are falling out of love. This can result in the "I love you but I'm not in love with you" syndrome, which is another sure sign that you have moved into the second stage of love. Rest assured the post-rapture period is not the death knell of romance; on the contrary, it is the beginning of true love. This book is designed to guide you through this stage and highlight the important lessons that will help you create the relationship you long for.

UNDERSTANDING THE NATURE OF POST-RAPTURE

Most couples have a period of romantic intensity when they fall in love, but within a few months are completely on their own as the high subsides. Research, as well as experience, show that a normal period of neutrality sets in between two people some time between six months and the second year of intimate contact. Neuroscientists theorize that the brain cannot eternally maintain its revved-up, lust-crazed state, either because the nerve endings become habituated to the brain's natural stimulants, or because levels of PEA and related substances begin to drop. If infatuation is chemically analogous to an amphetamine jolt, it makes sense that lovers develop a tolerance for each other over a period of time. And, just in practical terms, how long can two people go on staying up late, avoiding other responsibilities, keeping themselves secluded, and focusing solely on one another?

Understandably, as time passes, the novelty begins to wear off. Once you have sufficiently discovered one another and there are few surprises left, familiarity sets in. Whatever the precise cause of the retreat from infatuation, most of us have experienced this downshift in energy. Sooner or later, euphoria sneaks out the back door and reality makes its entrance, signaling the onset of the next stage of love. While some find this period more comfortable, others, seduced by the early excitement, find it disappointing. Even though this stage can be threatening, this is not the time to break up—it's a chance to break through!

If I could make one change in how the Western culture views relationships, I would change the perception that infatuation equals love. I have seen more heartache and disappointment come from this misconception than all others. Without a thorough understanding of infatuation and the subsequent Post-Rapture Stage, couples are at high risk. Given the fact that happiness is the ratio between what you expect and what you get, couples who don't realize that the waning of infatuation is normal are prime candidates for serious dissatisfaction.

Shana and Mac could have let a beautiful relationship slip away had they not understood the nature of the Post-Rapture Stage of love. The two of them had met through mutual friends when they were in their late twenties and each starting to get established. Neither of them had much money; therefore, even though their love was strong and there was a great attraction between them, they knew that marriage was out of the question for quite some time.

The early months of their relationship were intense—lots of late nights, long conversations, great sex, and high energy. But over time the demands of work had to be met, as well as personal obligations and responsibilities. Their limited budget restricted their activities and they knew that if they were going to be able to afford to be together, each had to give a lot of attention to their job in order to advance and make more money.

As the initial high wore off, they were faced with the reality of the Post-Rapture Stage. At first Shana was disappointed. When the euphoria wore off, she began questioning their relationship. She even began to fantasize about a former boyfriend and wonder if leaving him had been the right decision. But with calm reassurance from Mac, she made the adjustment to post-rapture and three years later, when finances enabled them to wed, they came to the altar not in the infatuated state but with a true love that has since stood the test of time.

The Post-Rapture Stage brought Shana and Mac the first serious challenge for their relationship. Fortunately, when Shana lost heart, Mac came forward with support and reassurance. Navigating this low time gave strength to their relationship and they have since weathered many low periods in their marriage. Each challenge they have faced has deepened their love.

QUICK FIX

If you have hit the wall and are stuck in the doldrums of post-rapture, the antidote might be quite simple: think back on the Infatuation Stage; recall what you did then, and start doing it again. When you were infatuated you paid attention to one another's needs and focused on pleasing each other. If you intentionally do this now on your own, it can have a delightful effect. You can bring back those loving feelings by acting in a loving way. If you want to feel romantic, be romantic. I know this takes dedication; however, it can have a great payoff and will help move you through the low spots of this stage. Try this experiment: right now start looking at your partner with the eyes of love. Flirt with him/her. Go out of your way to be sweet and thoughtful like you did in the early days. Do this as you go about your daily routine. This won't take any extra time, but you will be surprised at the effect!

THE LAZY LIBIDO

There are some challenges common to the Post-Rapture Stage that can't be resolved by simply going back to the practices of the Infatuation Stage. A waning of sexual interest falls into this category. Here's why. In the beginning of your relationship, Mother Nature is bound and determined for you to meet, mate, and procreate, so she uses the love cocktail to raise your libido. She gives you the biggest sexual urge in the first few months of intimacy, but then slowly withdraws the concentration as time goes by. By the second year, you are on your own without the aid of the love potion. Once this happens, your sex drive goes back to normal, or your previous level of sexual interest. For some people, normal sex drive means you want sex a lot; for others, normal means you don't want sex much at all. Whether high or low, each level of sex drive is natural and is not the result of the quality of the relationship. Scientists have known for decades that male sex drive is correlated with testosterone, which is a hormone produced in the testes and adrenals. While testosterone has been conclusively shown to highly correlate with male libido, it was long dismissed as a factor in the sex drive of women. Then in the early 1990s, Dr. Barbara Sherwin, a researcher at McGill University in Montreal, published her classic study showing that women who received a testosterone treatment reported a greater upsurge in sexual arousal, more lustful fantasies, a stronger desire for sex, more frequent intercourse, and higher rates of orgasm.

Subsequent research on women's naturally produced testosterone has yielded similar results. Women with high baseline levels of testosterone—so-called high-T women—tend to be significantly more sexually interested and responsive than low-T women. A substantial body of psychoendocrinological research has exploded decades of misunderstanding about female sexuality by establishing that libido requires a good supply of testosterone in women as well as in men.

Research linking hormone levels with libido has enabled us to further understand the phenomenon of infatuation. Let's say that a high-T person and a low-T person become attracted to one another (highly likely since opposites attract). During infatuation, with the help of PEA, dopamine, and norepinephrine, the person with the low sex drive (the low-T person) experiences a surge in sexual desire (see diagram). While under the influence of the love cocktail, the low-T person thinks, feels, and acts like a high-T person. This individual who ordinarily has little interest in sex, who is not easily aroused and doesn't think about sex, experiences just the opposite. On any given day, sexual fantasies, love play, and sexual initiation all become part of the infatuated behavior of the low-T lover, who is now believing "I have finally found someone who turns me on!" Meanwhile, the high-T partner is thinking, "I have died and gone to heaven. I have finally met someone who enjoys sex as much as I do." With this temporary infusion of amorous energy, the early months of infatuation are full of sexual intensity, as well as the joy of believing you have found the perfect lover.

It's important to realize that this period of increased erotic energy is a by-product of nature's time-limited plan. It is so delightful to have sexual desire if you haven't had any for a while. Wishful thinking makes one more inclined to draw the wrong conclusions. But PEA, like any other substance, loses its effect over time as you build up a tolerance to it. When this happens, each partner then goes back to his/her normal state. The low-T person returns to having little or no interest in sex, while the high-T partner stays quite interested. When the hormonal tide goes out and preexisting T-levels emerge, the "real" sexual partner is unveiled. At this point, both partners are apt to feel confused and disappointed. The high-T person, even without the infusion of the love cocktail, has a hormone level sufficient to still want plenty of sexual action, but the low-T person does not. The high-T person might feel betrayed, tricked, even cheated. Feelings of disappointment can lead to blame and accusations such as, "You've got energy for everything else but me." On the other hand, the low-T person may be totally confused and think, "I had it (libido) a couple months ago, where is it now?" Trying to comprehend the change, the low-T person might offer plausible reasons, "If you touched me more, spent more time with me (loved me, talked to me more, and so on), I would be more responsive." Deep down, the low-T partner also feels disappointed, inadequate, and maybe scared.

The problem is that the spike in sexual interest that accompanies infatuation can lead us to believe it will always be this way, but for most of us it will not. This is just a stage we are going through. After the inflated high during which both partners have a lot of sexual energy, each person then goes back to normal. This creates what is known as desire discrepancy, which is cited in the professional literature as the most common sexual dysfunction. I think it is unfortunate that desire discrepancy is classified as a sexual dysfunction because this is the norm for most couples. It's unrealistic to expect two people to have the same desire level given their biological differences. We need to understand that desire discrepancy mainly has to do with biology and your genetic makeup. Without this knowledge and understanding, individuals can end up confused, angry, and stuck in post-rapture disappointment. Take heart. There are many ways to move beyond this stage. Here are some useful suggestions.

TIPS FOR THE LAGGING LIBIDO

Since Nature selects for diversity, it is likely that at some point— or at every point—you and your partner will experience a difference in your desire for sex. This is a normal occurrence and is best addressed with acceptance and personal commitment. The discovery section of this book will help you decide just how important sex and romance are to you, and your relationship. But for now, I'd like to give some general direction for getting out of any sexual slump you may be experiencing due to the Post-Rapture Stage. First, and foremost:

Ask not only what is best for you, but also what is best for the relationship. This is a recommendation you are going to hear throughout this book. Periodically, and especially during difficult times, ask yourself, "What is best for the relationship?" This suggestion is especially relevant to sex. Given the fact that there will always be differences between any two people, keeping the health and welfare of the relationship in mind is essential. A loving heart challenges us to ask not only, "What do I want?" but "What is best for us?" Doing the right thing isn't always what comes to mind when you're in a relationship low spot, but looking at the big picture will likely give you the best perspective for making important decisions. (You probably don't enjoy paying your monthly bills, but thinking of what is best in the long run lets you see it's best for your credit rating and your peace of mind.) When you are striving for a satisfying sex life, you've got to keep sight of your ultimate goal—not just what you may be inclined to do at that moment.

Be a consumer activist for your sexual health. Sex is not just good for your relationship; it's good for you. The rhythmic activity stimulates the heart and increases blood flow throughout your body, fostering greater strength, flexibility, and stamina. It also sends the message to your brain "I am young and alive!" Loving sexual contact can elevate your mood by producing endorphins. It reduces tension and makes your body more relaxed. You also feel more connected to your partner if you share the joy of sex. Here's how it works. The hormone that triggers orgasm is oxytocin. You may have heard this familiar neurotransmitter referred to as the "snuggle chemical" because it is released when a mother breast-feeds, causing her to bond to the infant. It has the same effect on two people when they have sex. The release of oxytocin at the point of orgasm causes you to bond with your partner. This experience can be so powerful it can move you to tears.

Do what it takes to maintain a positive attitude about sex. Given the fact that the brain is the greatest sex organ, your attitude about sex is important and will affect your entire relationship. How you feel about yourself, your lovemaking, and your partner all have an impact on you as a lover. So first, think about what you need to do to feel good about yourself. You not only deserve this personally, but it is the surest way to make an overall improvement in your relationship. Second, ask yourself: "What do I need to do to feel better about my partner?" Improving your attitude can improve his/her behavior. And finally, check out what it is that would make you feel better about your lovemaking. What do you need to do to be a better lover? Improvement is contagious. Your excitement can expose you both to the love bug.

Make sex a priority. Once you have determined that sex is important to you and your relationship, put it at the top of your priority list. Make time for sex play. Create private moments for sex. Advocate for your sexual needs. Let your partner know how important making love is to you. Even though you might not need foreplay to become sexually aroused, this may not be true for your partner. Pay attention to creating a romantic atmosphere for sexual excitement.

Understand that low desire is often not a reflection of your relationship. Low desire can be the result of any number of causes, and most are not a commentary on the relationship. The most common cause of reduced sexual desire is hormone level. Just knowing that your lack of desire is connected to your physiology can take away the shame and blame that often accompanies lower libido. It is also important to look at other possible causes. For example, we know that many antidepressants lower sexual desire and responsiveness. Some antiulcer drugs interfere with testosterone and cause libido and erection difficulties. Prostate shrinkers lower the level of testosterone in some men. Some forms of birth control pills can lower sexual desire. Antihistamines can constrict arteries and block the flow to erections and lubrication. Sleeping pills can interfere with deep sleep in which sexually rejuvenating nocturnal erections occur.

Sometimes, the problem isn't with a single medication but an interaction between two or more medications taken in combination. Alcohol, drugs, and smoking can inhibit your sexual pleasure and performance. Low sexual desire can also be an early symptom of disease, such as diabetes or arteriosclerosis. As always, communication with your doctor is important in finding a solution. Ninety-nine percent of all sexual problems are treatable.

Understand that high sex drive can be normal for women as well as men. If you have never had a high sex drive, it is easy to misunderstand the needs of your high-T partner, or to overlook the fact that daily desire for sex is not uncommon for him or her. This doesn't mean that the two of you will be sexual every day, but the desire may still be there. This is normal and natural for someone with a high level of testosterone. Without this recognition, there may be a tendency to pass judgment or disapprove of a perfectly normal characteristic. Understanding and respect can go a long way toward creating happiness with your high-T partner.

Accept the sexual differences between you and your partner. A major characteristic of happy couples is they see lovemaking as an expression of intimacy, and they don't take the difference in their needs or desires personally. True love requires two mature people who can relate to one another, even when needs differ from their own. For example, a low-desire person may need a lot of loving contact to motivate him/her to put forth the effort it takes to be sexual. This is not the experience of a high-desire person, who does not have to work at getting aroused. A high-desire person can have sex when angry, tired, suffering from a headache, or having a bad hair day. This is not the case for the low-desire person. Keep in mind, each partner has a different set of needs. Consequently, it is important to be able to get out of your own frame of reference for a period of time. Accept these differences and work with them.

Communicate your sexual needs. If frequent sex is important to you, communicate this fact honestly and directly to your partner. You might be surprised at how many individuals have never been forthcoming with this information. Frequently, when I work with couples I have to say, "Tell your partner how important sex is to you." It's easy for your partner to ignore your needs if you haven't been clear and direct. Likewise, if you need a certain type of fore-play to be aroused, it is your responsibility to negotiate for this. It is especially important if your needs have changed. A significant percentage of the couples I see are stuck in a low spot in their sexual relationship because they need to do something different. They have difficulty knowing what they want and asking for it. It's important for the two of you to work together as a team around the issue of changing sexual needs because if you stay together long enough, you will need different sexual stimulation. Now's the time to start communicating more clearly.

Be willing to give and receive sex as a gift. Loving sex is good for you physically, mentally, and emotionally. Regardless of this fact, if neither of you is interested in being sexual and you're not hav-ing sex, there is no problem. But if one of you is interested, then to be satisfied you both need to be involved. Many times, I have seen couples come in for help with an unspoken and unworkable contract that goes something like this: "I expect you to be monog-amous, but don't expect me to meet your sexual needs." This is not a satisfying setup.

So, what should be done if one wants sex and the other doesn't? First, ask the basic question: "What is best for the relationship?" Second, think of sex as an investment in the relationship. A gift to your partner may need to be the motivation for the person who infrequently experiences sexual desire.

Many times I hear from the high-T person, "Well, I only want sex if my partner wants it like I want it." This is another unwork-able contract. It is normal for a low-T individual to have little sexual interest past the Infatuation Stage. However, even with a low-T level, you can be an incredible sex partner when inspired by the desire to give and receive pleasure. In order for this to work, the high-T person must be able to accept that the low-T partner is going to be motivated out of love and dedication to the relationship, not necessarily out of physical need or sex drive. The high-T individual must also understand that it takes a lot of effort and concentration for the low-T partner to become aroused and get in the mood for sex. In other words—it's work. Therefore, it's up to the high-T person to give this partner a reason to put forth effort. It's like the low-T person is saying "Give me something to work with. Help me get motivated toward sex." This can be anything from helping out with the children, to giving compliments, to using the proper sexual foreplay.

Sometimes I hear from the unsatisfied low-T individual, "Well, why should I do something when I don't feel like it?" The answer: "Because true love isn't just about me. It's about we."

The highs and lows of sex can be navigated by the two of you coming up with a win-win plan—and using love and kindness while doing it. For example, my husband and I have a distinct desire discrepancy. I'm low-T; he's high-T. To me, seasonal sex, i.e., once every summer, fall, winter, and spring, sounds good. His preference is the opposite. So, we came up with a plan in which he decides "when," and I decide "how." I can choose a quickie, a more leisurely encounter, or a sexual marathon. He's happy, I'm happy, and our relationship is happy.

One last comment: sometimes it helps to step back to an objective position and look at the facts. Mutually respectful sex between two consenting adults in a committed love relationship is a normal request and expectation. To reiterate: the truth about sex is it's good for you. It's good for your partner and—most important—it's good for your relationship. This ten- to twenty-minute investment goes a long way toward creating harmony and is a vital part of true love.

THE HIGHS AND LOWS OF LOVE

If you will recall, one of the side effects of PEA—nature's love potion—is the lowering of defenses. This means that during the Infatuation Stage you and your partner—without resistance—feel comfortable talking and listening, touching and being touched, being thoughtful, asking for and receiving help, expressing thoughts and feelings, spending private time together, and being sensual and sexual. In other words, you are being intimate and feeling the natural high that comes from it. However, after the effects of PEA are no longer being felt, you and your partner go back to your former behavior. The introvert talks less, and the pragmatist quits bringing flowers, and so on. And all of a sudden, time is of the essence; each of you has to catch up on the parts of your lives you've been neglecting since you met. There are friends to visit, duties to perform, and, of course, the ever present demands of work. Even though these changes are understandable and normal, they still come as a disappointment and create a low spot in the relationship. Common sense tells us that a love relationship, just like other relationships, has normal highs and lows; however, when the low times come, as they always will, it causes concern. Because a love relationship is so connected to our sense of security, any threat or change in it creates anxiety, and individuals handle it in various ways. The classic methods for managing anxiety include variations on the themes of fight and flight, that is, taking action or withdrawing. If you are not familiar with the truth about love, when the low spots come, you may manage your disappointment by pursuing, or distancing—the two classic ways of managing your anxiety. Neither of these styles leads to true love. To understand why, let's take a closer look.

PURSUING AND DISTANCING

When Marla gets concerned about their relationship, she moves in closer to Jack. As a pursuer, she commands more time, attention, or information. Pursuers tend to talk more, ask more questions, and are highly sensitive to any form of ignoring or rejection. (Ironically, their pursuing behavior evokes rejection.) Distancers do just the opposite. For instance, when Jack gets anxious, he gets quiet and focuses on something else. He seeks out time alone and can even ignore the problem. Distancers want to go at their own speed, which is rarely fast enough for the pursuer. They are highly sensitive to any action that feels like they are being controlled. (Of course the distancer's withdrawal invites control.) If Jack says anything at all it will most often be to ask Marla for patience.

When these pursuing and distancing behaviors show up, it's a sure sign you have made it to the Post-Rapture Stage. The effective way to manage these styles is to learn from one another. Because the pursuer's style is to complain and the distancer's style is to withdraw, in a nutshell: pursuers need to shut up and distancers need to show up!

This means the pursuer needs to learn from the distancer how to be more accepting, show patience, and focus on the positive aspects of the relationship. Because pursuers are wired to see what they are not getting, they tend to criticize, nag, whine, and complain, which just drives the distancer further away. The quickest way for a pursuer to move out of the post-rapture power struggle is to show appreciation for what is given.

Since distancers are wired to seek control, they tend to get rigid, intellectualize, stonewall, resist, and minimize problems. The quickest way out of the power struggle for the distancer is to speak up when dissatisfied, be forthcoming with time and attention, and make sure to show love in the specific ways the pursuer requests. The Post-Rapture Stage can elicit alarm and easily set into motion these pursuing and distancing behaviors. Incidentally, we are all capable of playing each of these roles, and it is not unusual to switch, depending on the context. For example, someone may be a pursuer in the living room and a distancer in the bedroom. Someone who withdraws when the conversation turns to feelings may pursue when the subject is money. Neither style is conducive to true love.

POST-RAPTURE AND OLD IMPRESSIONS

Throughout our lives we are constantly taking in information about the nature of relationships. Interactions with parents, family members, siblings, peers, and the culture at large form our image of relationships, as well as love. Therefore, when we go looking for a partner, we unconsciously look for familiar characteristics that fit our image of a lover. For example, Joanne's mother was a very patient woman, and it is no coincidence the characteristic that Joanne first noticed about her husband, Bob, was his patience with co-workers in the office. She was further touched by this quality on their first date. When she kept him waiting forty minutes, he sat calmly watching television and playing with her cat. If you look at the characteristics you admire in a love partner, you will find that they have been part of your past—and part of your image of love. We form our impressions, as well as our expectations of love, from our early experiences. Then later in life when we meet someone who matches our image, we are attracted because it feels like love to us. If this person is also a biological match, then we are likely to fall in love.

But given the fact that most of our early impressions of love came from human beings, it stands to reason that some of our interactions with the people who loved us were negative rather than positive. This being the case, we can also associate negative characteristics with love because they feel familiar. In the Infatuation Stage, you tend to focus more on your partner's positive characteristics and ignore the negatives. Under the influence of the love cocktail, you see through rose-colored glasses. Even when a negative trait becomes evident, you give it a positive spin. But in the Post-Rapture Stage it's a different story. Without the euphoria, negative traits become more evident. And if your partner has a negative trait that one of your caregivers had (and this will likely be the case), you will be hypersensitive to it and even be inclined to see it when it is not there.

Susan grew up with a controlling stepfather and her mother did little to protect her against his overbearing attitude and strict rules. When Susan married Julian, who had a five-year-old daughter, many of the arguments between him and Susan came from Susan's belief that Julian let his ex-wife control their family. If Julian had any contact with his ex, despite the fact that it was only about arrangements for their child, Susan went ballistic. After a particularly nasty argument, the two of them sat down, and through tears and anguish Susan began to share with Julian what it was like as a child to live with a controlling person with whom she had no power. Understanding her past helped Julian be more sensitive to Susan's need to be involved with all the decisions that affected their family. His sensitivity and support enabled Susan to see that his ex-wife's involvement was normal in a stepfamily, and eventually their relationship became a healing experience for Susan's past as well as their marriage.

Jeremy met Megan six years after a painful divorce from a woman who had been unfaithful to him. During their courtship and the infatuation period, Jeremy was happier than he had been in years. But as soon as the post-rapture period began and Megan started to attend to some responsibilities other than their relationship, Jeremy became extremely jealous and accused Megan of infidelity. At first Megan was patient and reassuring, believing that time would build trust between them. But Jeremy's jealousy became too disruptive to the relationship and when he refused to seek help or make any changes, they went their separate ways.

Quite often negative perceptions from the past fuel the disappointment of the Post-Rapture Stage of love. When the high wears off and the first lull occurs, it's easy to misunderstand this stage and jump to negative conclusions. It is part of human nature to try to make sense out of our circumstances. Accepting that post-rapture is normal can help you make sure that your past disappointments don't spoil your present.

MANAGING NEGATIVE TRAITS IN YOUR PARTNER

Try this exercise: write down the three characteristics of your partner that you would like him/her to change, i.e., that you don't like.

1.

2.

3.

Now, look at the characteristics you just listed. Ask yourself: when and how do these characteristics show up in me? If you can't come up with an answer, ask your partner. He or she will gladly tell you.

One effective way to handle perceived negative traits in your partner is to take ownership. Here's how it works. When you see a trait in your partner that you don't like, before you blame him/her, ask yourself this question: "How am I like that?" We tend to dislike and be hypersensitive to the traits in our partner that also live within us. It may not look the same, but if you take a thorough inventory, you will find it. Another way of dealing with your partner's negative characteristics is to see what you can learn from them. We tend to react to traits in others that we have trouble incorporating in our own lives. For example, you might resent the fact that your partner spends so much time with her friends. But the reality is, you could benefit from spending more time with your friends—or developing new friendships.

Finally, you might also look at how you provoke this negative trait or reaction in your partner. If you don't like your partner's defensiveness, check to see if you criticize, for defensiveness is the natural response to criticism. Likewise, if you cling, your partner will pull away. If you nag, you'll likely get procrastination. If you discount your partner, you will get anger and resentment. If you ignore his/her needs, you will likely get your needs ignored, too. If you are too busy too long, your partner may ulti-mately turn to outside sources of comfort and support.

The only surefire way to change or improve your relationship is to focus on your own behavior. As long as you are blaming or focusing on your partner's negative traits—as opposed to learn-ing from them—you are keeping true love at bay. When you change your behavior, you change the relationship. Your love life will not stay the same if you change.

LESSONS FROM THE POST-RAPTURE STAGE

The second stage of love has many valuable lessons, as well as op-portunities. First, it gives you a chance to truly know yourself—as well as your partner—without the influence of the love cocktail. Even though infatuation is incredibly delightful, it does not provide an accurate image of what the two of you are like in the real world of love. The Post-Rapture Stage provides an op-portunity to quietly assess the status of your relationship. You can look at your strengths, as well as your need for course correc-tions. Think of it as a "you are here" point on the map, with true love as your destination. Then ask, "What do I need to do to help us get there?"

Take a moment to look at the potential of your current rela-tionship. What are the positives? What special skills do you and your partner possess that can get you through the inevitable low times? What do you admire about your partner? What activities do you enjoy? What goals do you share? What memories from the Infatuation Stage can you carry with you as a reminder of your love and dedication? How can you use these memories to sweeten your journey?

Now look at yourself through the realism of the Post-Rapture Stage. What kind of a partner are you? Are you a fair-weather lover who is ready to withdraw or cast blame at any given low spot? Do you overreact to characteristics in your partner that have been part of your past? Post-rapture shows what kind of grit you have when it comes to true love. It reminds you that love is not infatuation. Real love has natural highs and lows and happiness comes from treating one another in a loving manner through it all.

An important truth to learn now is that it is much easier to keep a relationship satisfying or turn a low into a high if you pay attention to one another's needs. A rule of thumb to remember is that, for each negative thought or behavior in your relationship, it takes at least five positives to restore the satisfaction level. The Post-Rapture Stage becomes a danger zone when negative interactions start to overwhelm the relationship. You can use the strategies learned in this chapter to keep your ratio tipped to the positive side.

Even though the road can be rough in the Post-Rapture Stage, it is well worth traveling. What lies at the end is a life-sustaining connection with your partner, which is one of life's most precious experiences. No matter how long you have been in the Post-Rapture Stage, this book will provide the means for you to move safely on to the next stage, Discovery, and on to a satisfying connection. Despite how threatening this stage can be, take comfort in the knowledge that getting through each low spot will strengthen your love and deepen your satisfaction.

3

The Discovery Stage: Gathering Information

The truth about love is that it is ever changing. Throughout the life of a relationship, individuals change and life itself changes. Love has to be flexible enough to accommodate new information, new roles, and new ways of loving one another. Most low spots in relationships occur out of a need for discovery. If couples do not make a practice of examining current needs and making adjustments, they get stuck in a rut that offers little or no reward. The discovery process can transform the low spots in your relationship and give clear direction for creating the love you long for. Navigating the stage of Discovery for the first time in a relationship can be challenging as well as exciting. The next few chapters will take you through the exhilaration of discovering yourself, as well as your partner, on the journey toward true love.

THE BEGINNING OF DISCOVERY

If you have navigated the Post-Rapture Stage of love, you have probably adjusted your expectations somewhat and are seeing your relationship with an open mind. This primes you for the discovery period, a time in which you will begin gathering information about yourself and your partner and how the two of you want to be together in the real world. Since love does not mean the same thing to every individual or to every couple, only by surveying your needs and your partner's needs can you define your own unique form of love. Taking time for discovery helps you determine what you each want from the relationship. This process can be full of surprises and it isn't always easy. But with this book as your guide, I think you will find it a delightful experience.

THE IMPORTANCE OF GATHERING INFORMATION

Couples who rush through discovery, skipping over the information-gathering process, decrease the likelihood of their relationship going the distance and creating a love that lasts. Making a commitment while still in the Infatuation Stage—before you experience the realism of post-rapture or take the journey into discovery—can easily result in a regretful decision. In the throes of romantic love, information doesn't sink in. You need ample time and experience after the euphoria subsides to get an accurate picture of your partner, and ascertain if the two of you have shared values and the desire for the same type of relationship. Look at these examples of couples who skipped this important stage.

- Delene and Clark met and fell in love while working for the same company. Their relationship developed quickly because they spent time together at work as well as after hours. From the beginning, they were very attracted to one another and extremely compatible in their likes and dislikes. Problems came when the initial high wore off and they each went back to the former routine of their demanding jobs. They each were preoccupied with work and neither of them was planning special times together, giving thoughtful gifts, or creating romantic interludes. No one was minding the relationship; as a result, there was little love energy between them. Before long they were acting more like colleagues than lovers. They hadn't taken time to decide how the relationship was going to keep its romantic energy. They erroneously assumed loving each other would be enough. It wasn't.

- Eighteen months after her marriage to Alex, Serena found out that he had $8,000 in credit card debt. In the eight months she had known him prior to their wedding, she had never asked about his financial status, and in retrospect could plainly see that he had been living above his (and their) means. Alex felt comfortable with ongoing debt and held the belief that it was his debt and not a concern of their relationship.

- The first time Fred's two children visited him and his fiancée, Margarita, it had not gone well, but he assumed that everyone was just nervous. By the next visit he and Margarita were married. To his dismay, she was resentful and critical throughout the children's stay. The morning the children were to leave, she told the oldest child, Claudia, age eleven, that they were not to come again for at least a year. The marriage didn't last that long.

- Connie and Billy Bob had met at Club Med in early November. By January Connie had moved to Minneapolis from Chicago to be closer to him and they were married in July of that year. When the December holidays rolled around, Connie wanted to plan to spend some time with her folks and extended family. Billy Bob flatly refused, stating that he had never spent time away from his family during December and that they were to continue that family tradition as a couple.

- Rosie and Donald met at a friend's wedding shortly after he had moved to the D.C. area. Knowing that Donald was strapped for money while looking for a job, Rosie invited him to move in with her. She found it helpful having Donald at home, given her busy work and travel schedule. Initially he ran errands, cooked, even did the laundry. This support was such a comfort to Rosie it was easy to ignore the months that passed without him gaining employment. They were so compatible as lovers they began to talk of marriage, but Rosie insisted they wait until he found a job. Within two weeks of that discussion, Donald took a position with an advertising agency and in celebration they set the date for the wedding two months later. One month after the honeymoon Donald came home and announced he had quit his job. This was the beginning of the sporadic work history he maintained for the remainder of their relationship.

These individuals did not take time for the all-important period of discovery nor did they have the opportunity to learn the skills necessary to navigate the highs, lows, and rough spots of love. When their relationship hit its first crisis, they were already playing with high stakes—they'd moved in, they'd married, they'd invested in a relationship that was largely an unknown quantity. It is surprising how many clients have told me, "I knew it was wrong before I ever got married, but I went ahead and did it anyway because I thought it would get better." Relationships don't get better until you learn how to make them better. It's never too early or too late to learn the skills of gathering information and the sooner you learn, the closer you will be to creating true love.

GATHERING INFORMATION ABOUT YOU

When individuals answer "no" to the question: "Are you getting your needs met in your relationship?" and I ask "Why?" they often blame their partner. Most people take little or no responsibility for the fact that their needs go unmet. This is not the way of true love. Your needs are going to change—your partner's needs are going to change—so you both need a way of letting each other know so you can adjust your behavior accordingly.

LEARNING TO ASK

The first low spot in a relationship often occurs when it becomes necessary to communicate changing needs and expectations. Many of us have difficulty articulating what we want. It becomes even more difficult if you think your needs will not be met, or you are unsure of the validity of your expectations. The pain of living without may be perceived as less hurtful than the pain of being refused. Out of discomfort with asking, you might resort to the classic line: "Well, if I have to ask, just forget it!"

In the beginning of this book, I shared with you much of the distress and dissatisfaction I've had in a relationship. I am happy to say that today I am living with a satisfied heart. Even though the road from then to now has been long and full of lessons—some I had to repeat more than once—the outcome has been well worth the time and effort. Acknowledging my needs and having the courage to ask has been a large part of my journey because, at an early age, I had learned not to ask for anything.

As a child, I looked around at the people taking care of me and decided "these people have enough problems; I don't need to add to them" and I shut down my needs. This decision worked well in my family. I got rewarded for voicing few of my needs. My mother used to say, "You've never caused me a minute's trouble." I took this to mean, "Don't have any needs, and don't ask for anything." When I became a therapist I learned that I wasn't the only one who had difficulty asking. One client named Nicole had an older sister who was very demanding and selfish, so Nicole decided she did not want to be this way. She learned to ask for nothing. Crosby, on the other hand, grew up with a mother who anticipated his every desire, which precluded the need to ask. He grew up believing that if someone loved him, she would anticipate his needs and he wouldn't have to ask for anything. Jana's first husband ignored her needs, so she assumed her second husband would do the same. Before any of them could feel free to ask, they had to let history be history.

CULTURAL MESSAGES ABOUT ASKING

Sometimes cultural mores teach lessons about asking. I grew up in rural West Virginia, where there was very little money and most people were hard-pressed to provide for their families, let alone share with others. Because of this, the polite rule for visiting was: "Don't ask for anything." This is how it worked. If you went to someone's house for a visit, shortly after you arrived the hostess would say, "Can I get you something?" The ritual answer was, "No, no, nothing for me. I'm just fine, thanks." Then the hostess would come back, "Are you sure I can't get you a sandwich or something?" Your reply: "No, that's okay." But if she offered a third time: "I've got some tunafish salad in the refrigerator. Let me make you a sandwich," then you could say, "Okay, I'd love it." The translation of what was going on behind this colloquial ritual is this: The first offer "Can I get you something?" meant "Welcome to my home." The second offer "Are you sure I can't get you a sandwich or something?" translates "I am really glad you are here." Finally, the third offer "I've got some tunafish salad in the refrigerator. Let me make you a sandwich" meant "I do have enough food on hand and I'd like to share it with you." In retrospect, this ritual makes sense given the cultural environment. By refusing the first two offers and not asking for anything, everyone's dignity was kept intact. But it took me years to overcome this learned behavior and be able to ask, but when I did, my relationships became more satisfying.

RISKING REJECTION

You or your partner may have had early lessons that make it difficult for you to acknowledge your needs and ask for what you want. If so, then gathering information will be more stressful. But even if you weren't raised with prohibitive messages about asking, it can still be scary because, in asking, you risk rejection. Sometimes this fear of asking comes out as a criticism. More than once I have heard the man or woman say to the partner, "I have told you what I want over and over. I'm tired of asking. The real fact is you just don't care." My experience has been that the accusing partner is rarely innocent. Upon further investigation you may find:

- The request has not been specific. Example: "I want more intimacy" can mean any number of things. It may mean "I want more sex, touching, holding, talking about emotions, giving information, asking personal questions, flirting, and so on." The other person needs short, specific requests, such as, "I would like you to initiate sex at least once a month." Or, "Instead of going silent, I would like you to tell me when I've been rude to you."

- The request has been asked in a critical or blaming way, making it difficult to give generously.

- The person asking has been so unappreciative in the past that the partner has given up trying.

- The person making the request is unreasonable about expectations. She/he may expect the partner's paycheck to reflect overtime pay, for instance, but resent the fact that the partner works extra hours.

- The person making the request has been insensitive to the other partner's needs, thus making the relationship inequitable and the topic of giving a point of contention.

- The person asking has been so critical of previous efforts from the partner that resentment has built up and contempt and withholding have come into play.

Couples committed to creating true love have a clear, respectful, specific way of asking for what they want and need.

GATHERING INFORMATION ABOUT YOUR PARTNER

Love is not a one-way street. It's not just about getting your needs met; it's also about meeting the needs of your partner. The truth about love is that it comes from giving, as well as receiving. Much of the joy of a relationship comes from being generous. You feel good about yourself when you act in a kind and benevolent manner. The Discovery Stage is an important time to gather information not only about your needs, but also the needs of your partner. To help you do this, take a moment and ask yourself these questions:

Do I have a clear understanding of my partner's current needs?

Do I make an effort each day to meet my partner's needs?

Do I focus on pleasing my partner as much as I focus on being pleased?

Am I as sensitive to my partner's needs as I expect him/her to be to mine?

How do I respond when my partner expresses needs?

Would my partner say I make his/her needs a priority?

Do I make it easy for my partner to ask for what he/she wants?

During one of my couples workshops a few years ago, I divided the men and women into two discussion groups. My assistant led the men's group and I went to the women's group. The assignment was to talk about your sexual needs. During the course of the exercise, Sheila, a very bright, attractive blonde with the deepest turquoise eyes I've ever seen, was describing her painful relationship with her husband.

"He just turns away from me. I have tried everything—being affectionate, wearing sexy lingerie, cooking his favorite meals, trying to talk about our sex life—but nothing works. We haven't had sex for over two years. It's either that he just doesn't want sex, or he doesn't want me. I feel so unattractive, so inadequate. He's a good man and I love him to death, but I can't stand to think of living the rest of my life like this." Sheila dropped her head and began to cry. There was silence in the group; one of the women held her hand, another handed her a tissue. A couple of other women in the group offered support by describing similar disappointments. Then Linda spoke up in a strained voice.

"Sheila, as I was sitting here listening to you, my first thought was, 'Well, you should just leave him!' Then it hit me. I am just like your husband. I haven't given any thought to my partner's needs."

By listening to Sheila, Linda got an objective look at her own behavior, which is an important step in discovery. She had what I call a TMM—a temporary moment of maturity. This is a rare experience when, in an instant, you get a glimpse of what it is like living with you. Once you get this clear insight, your perception can never be the same. Once she heard Sheila's story, Linda would be unable to go on blindly ignoring her partner's needs.

What kind of partner are you? What is the view like from your partner's vantage point?

Given the fact that it is far easier to see our partner's faults than our own, it might be helpful to look at the following Personal Report Card, to see how well you fare in your relationship.

PERSONAL REPORT CARD

In terms of meeting your partner's expectations, how would you rate yourself in the following categories? Circle the number that best represents your answer.

1. Making time for our relationship.

Needs Improvement			Fair	Very Good	
1	2	3	4	5	6

2. Meeting my partner's sexual needs.

Needs Improvement			Fair	Very Good	
1	2	3	4	5	6

3. Making our relationship romantic.

Needs Improvement			Fair	Very Good	
1	2	3	4	5	6

4. Creating a loving family.

Needs Improvement			Fair		Very Good
1	2	3	4	5	6

5. Having a fair attitude about work.

Needs Improvement			Fair		Very Good
1	2	3	4	5	6

6. Being supportive with career issues.

Needs Improvement			Fair		Very Good
1	2	3	4	5	6

7. Giving and receiving physical affection.

Needs Improvement			Fair		Very Good
1	2	3	4	5	6

8. Initiating mutually satisfying intimate conversations.

Needs Improvement			Fair		Very Good
1	2	3	4	5	6

9. Being reasonable about money.

Needs Improvement			Fair		Very Good
1	2	3	4	5	6

10. Being a best friend to my partner.

Needs Improvement			Fair		Very Good
1	2	3	4	5	6

11. Being a good social partner.

Needs Improvement			Fair		Very Good
1	2	3	4	5	6

12. Interjecting fun into the relationship.

Needs Improvement			Fair		Very Good
1	2	3	4	5	6

13. Providing mental stimulation for our relationship.

Needs Improvement			Fair		Very Good
1	2	3	4	5	6

14. Doing my part in making a comfortable home.

Needs Improvement			Fair		Very Good
1	2	3	4	5	6

15. Being a good vacation buddy.

Needs Improvement			Fair		Very Good
1	2	3	4	5	6

16. Interacting with my partner in a kind, respectful manner.

Needs Improvement			Fair		Very Good
1	2	3	4	5	6

17. Being clear and trustworthy about my commitment.

Needs Improvement			Fair		Very Good
1	2	3	4	5	6

18. Spending time with friends in a way that is supportive of the relationship.

Needs Improvement			Fair		Very Good
1	2	3	4	5	6

19. Being a good partner around issues pertaining to children.

Needs Improvement			Fair		Very Good
1	2	3	4	5	6

20. Holding spiritual beliefs and practices that are conducive to strengthening the relationship.

Needs Improvement			Fair		Very Good
1	2	3	4	5	6

Total possible points: 120

Your total score: _____

*What I would add to this survey:*_____

*I feel good about:*_____

*Where I can most improve:*_____

Gathering information is not just important in the beginning of a relationship; it is imperative in an ongoing commitment. Fifty percent of people (most often men) report that their first indication the marriage was in trouble was when the partner said, "I'm getting a divorce." Now you know there were other signals before this, but the information was ignored. You have got to see with your eyes, hear with your ears, and feel what it's like to be in the relationship. If you want love to last, you can't be asleep at the wheel, especially during the low times, which offer some of our greatest learning opportunities.

Take the example of Alexia and Paul, who got to my relationship seminar just in the nick of time.

I noticed Paul before the one-day workshop even started because he was the tallest guy in the room and the only fellow with a ponytail and goatee. Alexia was a classic Italian beauty with a strong nose, full body, and dark, thick hair. During one of the breaks they came up and talked to me.

"Well, you ought to take this as a compliment," Alexia began, "because this is the first date we've had in over two years and we chose to come here. We both work. Paul has an eight-year-old son from his first marriage who's with us Wednesdays and every other weekend. We have two kids of our own—both in diapers—plus two dogs and a cat! There never seems to be enough time for just the two of us."

Then Paul spoke, "When we do interact with each other, we're at each other's throats. It seems like we are always fighting over the kids, over who didn't do what, you name it. When we do talk, it's mostly complaint. Lately, we've just been staying out of each other's way. But I know that isn't the answer. That's why we're here."

I was very glad Paul and Alexia had used their date time to come to my seminar. Any couple in their situation would find it challenging to juggle so many responsibilities. They would naturally need a lot of reassurance during this period, as well as some good, practical information. I touched base with them throughout the day and was moved by the work they were doing. At the end of the seminar, they came up to thank me and to make sure that I read their evaluation form. Here's what Alexia had written:

"This has been the best day we've had since our honeymoon! It felt so good just to focus on us. We learned that the low times we are going through now are NORMAL and that we really do have a strong relationship. We have rediscovered each other. We agreed that what's best for our relationship at this time in our lives is being good parents, restoring our sex life, and working as a team. I now understand how I have been ignoring Paul's sexual needs, and he understands that when he helps with the kids, I feel loved. We are committed to working with each other rather than against each other. And just letting each other know that we still love each other really helps. But most of all, we took time to remember all the things that satisfy us about our relationship. Thank you."

Alexia and Paul were experiencing a great deal of stress because of important demands during this period in their lives. But as they began to identify their needs, they realized that being a good parent was a priority to both of them and that they each felt loved when they worked as a team. In addition, they each identified a personal top priority need: for Paul it was sex; for Alexia it was a little more free time. Then they each acknowledged that they had not been sensitive to one another's personal needs. With new information, understanding, and a little course correction, they were able to restore their satisfaction.

The ongoing desire to please your partner and improve the relationship is a driving force behind successful marriages. Current research on happy, stable couples indicates one recurring theme: loving behaviors are what keep people together. They don't solve all their problems or stop arguing, but satisfied couples meet each other's needs in a positive way.

THE BRAIN'S SIGNAL FOR COURSE CORRECTIONS

Love is a response to having your needs met. When a partner meets your needs, the response is personal pleasure and fondness. If this continues, a bond develops and love is born. Out of love comes altruism, which is an unselfish desire to meet your partner's needs. This joyous flow of giving and receiving moves the relationship deeper into connection and creates true love. Yet anyone who has been in a satisfying relationship for a period of time will tell you there are highs and lows.

If for no other reason than because there are human beings involved, relationships go up and down. People change. Needs change. Let's face it: life itself brings change. Sometimes the relationship gets lost in the shuffle. But the human psyche is perfectly equipped to stay in tune with your needs and alert you when adjustments are necessary. When your relationship starts to get off course, the brain sends a signal telling you to alter your direction.

As we have seen, neurobiologists have identified the portion of our brain that serves as this internal navigator. The amygdala, which is an almond-shaped portion of the limbic brain, functions as an emotional alarm system by scanning incoming information for potential danger. When the information is perceived as threatening, such as "your needs are not being met," chemicals are released that cause portentous feelings like disappointment or frustration.

These so-called negative emotions are eloquently designed to get our attention so that we can make adjustments. Therefore, uncomfortable feelings that accompany the low spots in love are not tolling the end of love; they are simply signals telling us that change needs to occur. Just like road signs, the down times are designed to get us from where we are to where we want to be.

HAPPINESS IS THE RATIO BETWEEN WHAT YOU EXPECT AND WHAT YOU GET

The beginning of a relationship is filled with happiness. From his research, Dr. Larry Kurdek, Ph.D., from Wright State University observed that, "Most relationships start off with such high levels of quality that it can only go down." There are simple reasons for this. In the Infatuation Stage, you don't need much from your partner because you are basking in the pleasure of the chemical high. Also, new lovers spend an inordinate amount of time and energy trying to please one another, and, furthermore, very little is expected at the beginning of a relationship. With little or no expectation, every action, thought, or deed is experienced as a bonus, as well as a delight. A simple card, a little stuffed teddy bear, or a flower picked from the neighbor's yard can bring a thrill to your heart. (These tokens of love take on such meaning they are often saved for years.) A sweet phone call from your lover can keep infatuation going for days; however, over time as the relationship deepens, expectations change. If you have been dating someone for a year, one phone call won't go far. In fact, if that's all you get within the space of three or four days, it might irritate you.

Expectations change in direct correlation to the intimate nature of the relationship. For example, if your lover gives you chocolate-covered strawberries on your very first Valentine's Day, you might accept this as romantic and sweet. But if you get them after your lover knows you are allergic to strawberries, that's a different story.

Regardless of who is at fault, when you are not getting your expectations met, your partner can do very little to please you. Even the way he/she eats, snores, or folds clothes can annoy you. When your needs are ignored, there's no such thing as a little issue. Every frustrating event becomes further evidence for your dissatisfaction. When you argue, what you are arguing about is often not what you are arguing about. The subject may be turning off the lights, but the real issue is lack of emotional connection. When couples stay current with information about one another's needs and work together to meet those needs, this can take away many of life's daily irritations and make for a more satisfying home life.

LEARNING FROM DISTRESS

When needs go unmet, the relationship starts to show signs of distress. As disappointment grows, frustration may turn to criticism or withdrawal. If the negative interactions continue, the result may be defensiveness, and even contempt. When a couple resorts to these behaviors, common sense tells us the relationship is in trouble. Research backs this up. Dr. John Gottman and his researchers at the University of Washington found that nine times out of ten couples who criticize, get defensive, withdraw, blame, accuse, or call each other names do not make it. These habits constitute a dangerous low spot in a relationship.

A simplistic approach to correcting these bad habits might be to say, "Well, don't practice these behaviors." That's easier said than done because all of these behaviors cited by research as predicting divorce are just the symptoms. They do not reveal the root cause of the problem. The crucial questions are, "Why does Jennifer criticize?" and, "Why does Noel stonewall?"

We must look closer to discover the unmet needs behind these unsavory habits. Generally speaking, couples use destructive methods in their relationship because their needs are not being met. In order to avoid the interactions that take you further and further into the low spots, you must learn effective ways of gathering information about these respective needs. Ideally, you will begin to practice these skills in the earliest days of discovery:

- Being aware of your changing needs.

- Being willing to express your needs in an effective manner.

- Being sensitive to your partner's changing needs.

- Being flexible, i.e., willing to change as needs change.

- Accepting differences between your and your partner's needs.

- Accepting changes in your partner's needs.

- Making the needs of the relationship a priority.

Dissatisfaction is your brain's way of telling you it's time to make course corrections. All relationships must adjust to change over time. This is a normal part of any system. Here are some important signs to look for.

GATHERING INFORMATION FROM CRITICISM

Criticism is a sideways attempt to get your needs met. People who have difficulty or a fear of asking often resort to criticism. Pursuers are the guiltiest of using criticism because they have difficulty focusing on what they have; instead, they focus on what they don't have. Pursuers assume they are not going to get their needs met, and when they do, they're suspicious. Example: "Well, you came home early because your boss was out of town, not just to be with me." Pursuers are also hypersensitive to rejection, which increases the difficulty when asking for their needs to be met.

Many of us learned at an early age that negative behavior (yelling, calling someone names, and so forth) gets attention. We also learned that sometimes complaining gets your needs met. However, criticism is not mutually satisfying. It might give you temporary satisfaction—even attention—but it will not feel good to your partner or draw the two of you closer together.

When you criticize you don't act in the best interest of the relationship because it pushes your partner away. Criticism is a form of blame, which puts your partner on the defensive. It is also the opposite of ownership, and reinforces your belief that your partner is responsible for the difficulties in your relationship. To take full advantage of the Discovery Stage you need to look more closely at your own behavior.

IF YOU LOOK BEHIND CRITICISM, YOU WILL FIND A DESIRE

There is a simple way to short-circuit criticism: ask for what you want. Instead of "You never want to spend time with me!" say, "I miss you. I want to spend time with you." Both messages have the same intent but will elicit a very different outcome. You can also let your partner know what you want through compliments, such as a thank-you note or some other type of appreciation. These methods are far more effective and more satisfying. If your partner is criticizing you, instead of getting defensive ask, "How can I help?" It's impossible to have an argument unless you both participate. Responding to criticism with an offer to help is a quick way to shift the relationship to a more satisfying position.

GATHERING INFORMATION FROM WITHDRAWAL

While criticism represents the fight response in relationships, withdrawal represents the flight response. Withdrawal is another way of dealing with the fear of asking for what you want and letting others know how you feel. Distancers are experts at withdrawing from the relationship. They withdraw into work, television, hobbies, computers, activities, reading, and staying busy while all the time they long for connection. One classic distancer told me, "I love it when my grown children come to visit. I like sitting in the next room listening to them talk." Distancers want and need connection just as much as pursuers. This is an important point to remember because on the surface it doesn't look this way. And despite what they say, distancers like the feeling of being pursued because they desire connection. If you leave a distancer alone for long, he/she will find a way to get you to come closer. Distancers do not like to ask, so they stay at arm's length to get the other person to approach.

Distancers withdraw even further (sometimes they pout and storm around) if they believe their needs are not going to be met. The problem is, the partner is left in the dark not knowing how he/she might have contributed to the disappointment, or how to help. Sometimes the distancer in withdrawal assumes, "If you love me, you will know what I want." This is rarely true. Love doesn't make us mind readers.

Distancers are hypersensitive to criticism; they don't want to be told what to do or be seen as inadequate. At the first hint of disapproval, they disappear or get angry. If you recognize yourself as a distancer, the discovery process will include finding a way to speak up or express yourself, whether it is in a note, an e-mail, through a phone conversation, or face-to-face. Asking for what you want in a kind, respectful manner will help you and your partner design the relationship you long for and bring you closer to true love.

GATHERING INFORMATION FROM DEFENSIVENESS

Oliver was a CPA with aspirations of having his own accounting firm. He worked an average of sixty hours a week and most nights would come home exhausted. His pet peeve was walking in the door looking forward to a quiet night at home with his wife, only to find their three kids doing everything but what they were supposed to be doing. One particular night as he pulled into the driveway, he almost ran over Ollie Jr.'s bicycle, tripped on Jessica's backpack as he walked in the front door, and then found little Sereta running around the house stark naked.

"Jeannette!" he shouted, kicking the backpack out of his path as he went searching for his wife.

"Jeannette!" he yelled, even louder this time.

"Hi, Daddy," greeted Jessica as she walked through the room with the phone in her ear.

"Don't 'Hi, Daddy' me. Hang up that phone and pick up your backpack. Right now! And where's your mother?"

"I'm right here," Jeannette answered as she came down from upstairs. "What's all the yelling about?"

"Can't you control these kids? This place is like a zoo!" Oliver growled.

"Don't come in here and start in on us," Jeannette barked back.

"Jessica, didn't I tell you to pick up that backpack. Get over here right now!" he demanded.

"We were doing fine until you walked in with your bad attitude," Jeannette snarled while picking up the backpack.

With that, Oliver stormed into his office, slammed the door, and didn't come out until everyone had gone to bed.

When Jeannette responded in a defensive manner, she was joining the argument that was just waiting to happen. Defensiveness is a sure sign that a feud is about to occur. Criticism is usually the first blow, which is like saying "Do you want to fight?" Defensiveness is a definitive "Yes, you're on!" When ridicule is met with ridicule, no one wins and the relationship loses. As you can see in the scenario above, the criticism and defensiveness between Oliver and Jeannette affected the entire family. Research has shown that everyone in the household would have released stress hormones in response to that scene. Once your heart rate and blood pressure are elevated to the point of adrenaline release, it takes quite some time to come down from that rush of energy. There is also a hangover effect that stays with you.

For years therapists have approached anger with the attitude of "get it all out." However, research has shown that anger begets anger. The more you get angry, the more you get angry. Ironically, the more unreasonable and rude you get, the less others will take you seriously.

This isn't the case when you express your disappointment and frustration without yelling, criticizing, or being defensive. When you speak your mind with confidence, you get a lot more respect and more satisfying responses. Defensiveness can be a response to attack, but it can also come from the hopelessness of believing you will never be able to please your partner. When expectations are unclear or unrealistic and there has been little or no appreciation in response to efforts, then defensiveness is a natural recourse. This is why gathering information is so important in creating a satisfying relationship.

GATHERING INFORMATION FROM CONTEMPT

Contempt is the ultimate form of disrespect, which is not a part of true love. Whether it is name calling, sarcasm, ignoring, or making a "crime sheet" of your partner's faults, these forms of contempt will not satisfy either one of you in the long run.

Claire had a particularly harmful habit of ridiculing Charles in front of their friends, and yet she could not see the connection between this behavior and his withholding of affection, which she greatly resented. It took several sessions of therapy for Charles to express how humiliating it was for him to be criticized in front of others. For the past two years Claire had been angry with Charles because he had shown her no affection or support. Consequently, it took her quite a while to understand that she, too, was withholding—even contemptuous—with him. They each had to focus intently on what was best for their relationship, and take ownership of their individual styles of punishing one another, before they could move back to a place of love and connection. Any act of disdain or unkindness displays a negative attitude about your partner and takes away from relationship satisfaction. Respect, on the other hand—holding your partner in esteem and giving him/her courteous regard—forms the basis of a satisfying relationship.

THE FROZEN IMAGE—THE ULTIMATE FORM OF CONTEMPT

If you are in a relationship with a normal human being, there will be times when he or she will fall short of your expectations. But if you keep your eyes open—as well as your mind—you will likely gather enough information to see that most of the time your expectations are indeed being met, and that your partner is doing his/her best to satisfy you. But if you refuse to take in new information, you may end up with a frozen image of your partner, which can do great harm to the relationship.

If you've ever gotten off to a bad start with someone and then been unable to change that person's image of you—no matter how hard you tried—you know how frustrating this can be. When one partner forms a negative image of the other and is unwilling to consider new information that may contradict the bad impression, the relationship suffers. Willingness to update one's image helps to keep the relationship hopeful and alive. Most of the time this frozen image has its roots in childhood, when parents or other authority figures failed to meet the needs of the child. Ted and Trisha Nestor's story illustrates this point.

One Monday afternoon, I got a call from my publisher asking if she should give my phone number to a client who was seeking my help. I consented, and early Tuesday morning, Ted Nestor called requesting an appointment for him and his wife, Trisha. My schedule was quite tight and didn't fit with his, but he readily agreed to cancel a business trip to Europe to accommodate our getting together soon. After asking about possible bed-and-breakfast locations (he said this was his wife's preference), we set an appointment time and hung up.

The day of their appointment, Trisha came into my office first.

Ted arrived a couple minutes later carrying a fresh cappuccino he had picked up for her.

"So, how can I be of help?" I began.

Without looking at Ted, Trisha answered, "Well, our biggest problem is that Ted doesn't care about our relationship."

I looked at Ted, expecting a response. He was looking down at the floor.

"Let me see if I've got this," I replied. "Ted, you were the one who tracked me down through the publisher, right?"

"Yes," he answered.

"And then you called to schedule an appointment."

"Yes."

"And, Ted, you canceled your trip to Europe?"

"Yes."

"Did you make bed-and-breakfast accommodations?"

"Yes."

I looked at Trisha, who was drinking her cappuccino. "I'm confused. Is this the guy you say doesn't care about your relationship?"

The Nestors had been married for seventeen years and much of that time was fraught with difficulty. As we unraveled the issues, it became clear that each had a frozen image of the other. Early in life, long before they met, Ted and Trisha had formed a picture of love and marriage, which was still affecting the way they viewed each other today.

Trisha's father had been a cold, distant man who rarely interacted with the family. He went to his grave without ever clearly expressing his love for his children or his wife. Ted's mother and father divorced when he was eleven years old. Ted was left with a depressed father who later married a woman with two children of her own who never accepted Ted. These early experiences formed a frightening image of relationships for both Ted and Trisha. She saw men as uncaring; he saw women as unaccepting.

Early in their marriage they began to project these images onto one another.

To get a closer look at how I helped the Nestors and how you can check out any frozen image you might have about relationships, complete the following exercise.

THE FROZEN IMAGE

Think about your childhood and your earliest impressions of men and women in relationships. Use this perspective, as well as what you have learned from previous relationships and our culture, to complete the following sentences:

Men are_____

Women are_____

A woman's needs in a relationship are_____

A man's needs in a relationship are_____

When you commit to a relationship you_____

To get my needs met by a partner I must_____

Women always_____

Men always_____

The most powerful person in a relationship is_____

Being in relationship requires a woman to give up_____

Being in relationship requires a man to give up_____

Anger is_____

Silence is_____

Marriage is_____

Divorce is_____

As you look at your answers, ponder the following questions:

Can you see any similarities in your answers above and your perception of past or present relationships?

Can you see any connection between your answers and your perception of men and/or women?

Do your answers reflect any difficulties you've had in relationships?

Can you see how your expectations of men might affect your relationships?

Can you see how your expectations of women might affect your relationships?

Given your answers, what kind of relationship might feel familiar to you?

Right now, what do you think of men in general? How has that affected your relationships?

Right now, what do you think of women in general? How has that affected your relationships?

Looking at your answers, what fears might you have in relationships?

How has your behavior caused problems in your love relationships?

By answering these simple questions, Ted and Trisha could see how they had each brought a set of negative expectations into their marriage. When Ted's mother left his father, his dad, a successful hardware store owner, turned to work to manage his depression. Although he provided well for Ted and his second wife, he had little contact with the family. Ted had worked equally as hard as a businessman and as a husband. With each marital conflict, he had worked harder and harder to make Trisha happy. He gave her everything money could buy but, unfortunately, he didn't listen when she told him what she wanted was *him*. Her growing unhappiness fed his fear that she would ultimately leave, just as his mother had. He coped with his fear by working more.

Trisha's parents had lived in a traditional marriage with her mom as the homemaker and her father as an air force officer. She had seen her mother go weeks without much contact with her father. As a little girl, she missed her dad and never received enough time with him, even when he was home. Through this exercise, Trisha began to see how she had carried the resentment and loneliness from her childhood into her marriage and had expected all along that Ted would ignore the relationship. She easily believed that he did not care for her or their marriage. She handled her disappointment by withdrawing and complaining. Once Ted and Trisha could let go of the frozen images they had carried from childhood, they began to see each other in a new light. Ted could see that his wife really wanted time with him. Trisha could see that Ted truly cared for her, as well as their marriage.

TIPS FOR THE TOUGH TIMES

There are numerous lessons to be learned from the low times in a relationship. How you handle the tough spots largely determines whether you will experience true love. Plus, the specific behaviors we use during these times can be used as guidelines for transformation. In short:

- Instead of criticizing, ask for what you want. And when your partner criticizes, ask "What do you need?" and "How can I help?"

- When you find yourself getting defensive: Stop. Start over. Call time out. Apologize. Ask for more information. Take a deep breath.

- When your partner withdraws, give him/her more time and space. Find a way to manage your anxiety until the mood shifts. Entertain yourself. Do something fun. When you withdraw, let your partner know you need some time alone and about how long you need. If your withdrawal has nothing to do with the relationship, let this fact be known. If you have a problem, speak up.

- When there is contempt between the two of you, note this as a sign that the relationship could be in serious distress. Take time out to restore the good feelings between you. Do those activities that always work to bring you closer together. Seek help.

Working as a team when the going gets tough can deepen your love as well as your connection.

To determine how prepared you are to continue in the discovery process, see how well you fare on this quiz.

Answer T (true) or F (false) to the following statements:

_____ 1. I am kind and clear when expressing my needs.

_____ 2. I am sensitive to my partner's needs.

_____ 3. I rarely criticize my partner.

_____ 4. My partner would say I rarely criticize him/her.

_____ 5. I am comfortable asking for what I want in our relationship.

_____ 6. I am rarely defensive.

_____ 7. My partner would say I am good about meeting his/her needs.

_____ 8. I have great respect for my partner.

_____ 9. My partner would say I am a good communicator.

_____10. I am good about sharing information with my partner.

The ongoing desire to please your partner and improve the relationship is a driving force behind successful marriages. Current research on happy, stable couples indicates one recurring theme: loving behaviors are what keep people together. They don't solve all their problems or stop arguing, but satisfied couples meet each other's needs in a positive way. Since happiness is the ratio between what you expect and what you get, being clear about what you want and being willing to continuously take in and update information about one another will greatly improve your chances of living with a satisfied heart.

GATHERING INFORMATION ABOUT THE NATURE OF LONG-TERM LOVE

One fall day, my husband and I attended a wedding held on the Riverwalk in the heart of romantic San Antonio. It was a ceremony straight out of a storybook. A string quartet greeted us at the gate of a limestone courtyard and welcomed us to a canopy of huge trees. The ceremony was held in a gazebo wrapped in yards of white gossamer and garlands of jewel-toned flowers. We sat there enjoying weather so perfect it made you understand why Texans put up with the hot summers.

As the magic of the setting lured us into a reverie, a trumpet fanfare announced the arrival of a wedding party heretofore only imagined by *Bride's* magazine. Handsome men in black tuxedoes lined up to greet gorgeous bridesmaids floating in long gray satin dresses accented by bouquets of ruby-colored flowers. Then the bride arrived in such splendor she made you forget everything you had seen up to this point. The look on her face spread joy throughout the crowd and was only surpassed by the adoration of the groom. With misty eyes, we basked in their radiance as the minister inspired us with the nuptial service.

This ambiance continued into the reception and provided the perfect opportunity for me—ever the researcher—to ask people what they have learned about marriage. Somehow the euphoria of the ceremony, which reminded us of hopeful beginnings, also prompted us to remember the inevitable down times. The conversation began in a general manner but soon people, drunk with delight, were sharing their personal stories and philosophy.

Charlene, a charming woman from Tennessee, caught my interest with her comment, "I've divorced and remarried my husband four times in twenty-two years. We've never changed partners but have had four different marriages to each other."

"So what's your secret? How have you stayed together during the divorce times?" I asked, given it was clear she was happily married.

"Each time the marriage hit a standstill, one of us came to the other and said, 'Hey, this marriage isn't working for me. Here is what I'm needing from you now,' and every time, the other one was willing to change."

As Charlene's eyes filled with tears, I smiled at her in silent appreciation. She and her husband had not literally divorced. They had "divorced" the aspects of their relationship that were not working and had "remarried" by changing to meet each other's needs at the time.

Another woman, Mary Lou, observed, "Couples starting out in marriage today don't seem to understand that ups and downs are normal—that you've got to expect your relationship to change—and be willing to change with it."

Later, I was struck by the wisdom of these women whose combined fifty-plus years of marital experience were giving strong support to the case for flexibility, an important skill related to long-term love. As Charlene and Mary Lou attested, people change, and their relationship needs to be flexible enough to change with them. This fact seems obvious, but I have seen numerous couples struggle with their transitions. Many times I have heard one partner say to the other, "You weren't that way when I married you," implying that change is somehow bad or not normal. But life is one long series of changes, and satisfying love is sustained by staying abreast of change and adjusting to one another's mutable needs. Charlene and her husband kept love alive by making course corrections when needed, even if it meant completely redesigning their marriage. Mary Lou knew to expect highs and lows and wasn't shaken when they occurred. If you and your partner can learn these lessons in the early days of your relationship, then you will be another step down the road to true and lasting love.

4

Discovery: Clarifying Roles

Just a few decades ago, the subject of clarifying roles in a relationship would never have been included in a book about love because roles were predetermined. The male was expected to be breadwinner, provider, and protector. The woman was designated as homemaker, nurturer, and sex partner. Through the commitment of marriage, each was afforded long-term assurance that their respective needs would be met through these roles. The only aspect left to discovery was how well both people would perform their respective roles. During the latter half of the twentieth century, however, changes began to impact this traditional model of relationship and roles were called into question. Within a short period of time, the archetype we idealized in *Father Knows Best* and *Little House on the Prairie* represented the minority of U.S. families. Couples who commit to one another in the twenty-first century now have a much wider range of options, but the transition has been anything but smooth. Dissatisfaction and confusion plague couples who all too often believe their struggle is with each other when, in fact, they are really at odds with their respective roles. One woman might have said it best when she said, "I love my husband, but I hate my marriage." In this chapter, I will share with you the information that has helped a multitude of individuals clarify their roles only to find that happiness was waiting close by.

MEETING NEEDS THROUGH ROLES

As I've already said, happiness in a relationship is directly related to getting your needs met and meeting the needs of your partner;

however, time does not allow for negotiating every little move in our daily interactions. For this reason, couples assume roles. In an effort toward efficiency, they take on mutually agreed upon job descriptions. Once they come to an understanding about the role they each want the other to play, meeting needs becomes simplified. Fulfilling role expectations makes the relationship run more smoothly and the individuals happy. What most couples find when they hit a low spot is that one partner is not playing the role that the other expects.

When conflict occurs, they first need to gather information and then clarify their roles. The following pages are designed to help you do this—and avoid some of the greatest disappointments in love. Let's begin by looking at the three major relationship role models couples are choosing today—the traditional, the reverse traditional, and the neo-traditional.

THE TRADITIONAL MODEL

In this age-old paradigm, the day after the wedding the couple could slip right into their respective roles without much discussion or negotiation. The man went off to work; the woman began making a home. I was a full-time homemaker for many years in my first marriage, and I loved running the household. I worked hard, but I thoroughly enjoyed my job. At the time I often reflected how delightful it must be to have a wife—i.e., to have your clothes appear clean and pressed, to have meals prepared for you, and to always walk into a clean, tidy home. Years later when I went from being a homemaker to college professor, I wanted a wife! (I still do.) Despite the fact that today a minority of marriages are strictly traditional, every one of us has some semblance of this model in our heads. We have lived with it through our parents, grandparents, neighbors, friends, and the media. To understand how traditional your life is, complete the following survey.

THE TRADITION QUOTIENT

Circle the number of the answer that fits your experience in relationships. Tell it like it is, not like you might want it to be.

1. The woman is responsible for more than 50 percent of the housework.

Seldom		Some of the Time		All the Time	
1	2	3	4	5	6

2. The man makes more money than the woman.

Seldom		Some of the Time		All the Time	
1	2	3	4	5	6

3. The woman organizes most family activities.

Seldom		Some of the Time		All the Time	
1	2	3	4	5	6

4. The man initiates sex more often.

Seldom		Some of the Time		All the Time	
1	2	3	4	5	6

5. The woman initiates the intimate conversations.

Seldom		Some of the Time		All the Time	
1	2	3	4	5	6

6. The man has ultimate veto power over large purchases.

Seldom		Some of the Time		All the Time	
1	2	3	4	5	6

7. The woman is responsible for most social engagements.

Seldom		Some of the Time		All the Time	
1	2	3	4	5	6

8. Outside maintenance and lawn care is mostly the man's responsibility.

Seldom		Some of the Time		All the Time	
1	2	3	4	5	6

9. The woman is responsible for most of the at-home entertaining.

Seldom		Some of the Time		All the Time	
1	2	3	4	5	6

10. Major household repair is the responsibility of the man.

Seldom		Some of the Time		All the Time	
1	2	3	4	5	6

11. The woman makes most decisions about meals and food.

Seldom		Some of the Time		All the Time	
1	2	3	4	5	6

12. The man's job/career is seen as more important than the woman's.

Seldom		Some of the Time		All the Time	
1	2	3	4	5	6

13. The woman does the shopping.

Seldom		Some of the Time		All the Time	
1	2	3	4	5	6

14. The man shows interest in sex.

Seldom		Some of the Time		All the Time	
1	2	3	4	5	6

15. The man's job or career influences where the couple lives.

Seldom		Some of the Time		All the Time	
1	2	3	4	5	6

16. The woman is responsible for home decorating and style.

Seldom		Some of the Time		All the Time	
1	2	3	4	5	6

17. Both the man and the woman prefer the man to be the primary breadwinner.

Seldom		Some of the Time		All the Time	
1	2	3	4	5	6

18. The woman is more nurturing.

Seldom		Some of the Time		All the Time	
1	2	3	4	5	6

19. The man is more responsible for mechanical activities such as the car, tools, machinery.

Seldom		Some of the Time		All the Time	
1	2	3	4	5	6

20. The woman shows more emotion.

Seldom		Some of the Time		All the Time	
1	2	3	4	5	6

If applicable:

21. The woman spends more time with the children.

Seldom		Some of the Time		All the Time	
1	2	3	4	5	6

22. The woman is ultimately responsible for child care.

Seldom		Some of the Time		All the Time	
1	2	3	4	5	6

23. When a child is sick the woman is first to take responsibility.

Seldom		Some of the Time		All the Time	
1	2	3	4	5	6

24. The man's job commitment takes time from his parenting.

Seldom		Some of the Time		All the Time	
1	2	3	4	5	6

25. The man is the disciplinarian.

Seldom		Some of the Time		All the Time	
1	2	3	4	5	6

Total possible points: 150

Your total score: _____

75–150 = traditional model　　　*0–74 = nontraditional model*

It might be interesting for you to go back over the questions and mark your preferences to see if they differ from reality.

Anthropologists tell us that role division has been a part of our history as a species. Since the beginning of time, men and women have had their designated roles and used them to organize the culture. Let's take a look at some of the couples who are choosing the traditional model today.

THE UPWARDLY MOBILE MALE

A significant percentage of traditional marriages have a male who is an ample provider and prefers the wholehearted support of a wife who will love him and create a haven from the stresses of the outside world. He does not want the complexity brought about by two careers; instead, he wants a helpmate who will see his job or career as primary and play a strong part in making him a success. Being a father is often an important part of the traditional, career-driven man. Because providing financially is his top priority, he needs his wife to provide emotional support for the children and maintain a stable home life.

THE SECOND MATE

Women who are drawn to the traditional model expect the man to be the financial provider and appreciate the fact that they do not have to enter the outside world of work. Like the media image of Martha Stewart, women in traditional marriages often enjoy the role of homemaker and take pride in their domestic accomplishments. A significant number of these women have a deep need and desire to be a mother and consider this to be their finest role. They gain personal fulfillment from watching their children's accomplishments and feel gratification through providing a comfortable environment where they can grow and flourish.

THE HIGH-COST COUPLE

It's important to note that many couples choose the traditional model at considerable cost and personal sacrifice. They are willing to bear the financial burdens of living on one salary to uphold the values they share regarding marriage and family. Both husband and wife are willing to delay personal gratification to live in the model they believe in. In one newer form of marriage, the traditional model is regarded as an early chapter in the lives of the married couple. It is often chosen for the period of time when there are children at home. Sometimes women keep one foot in the career world by working part-time during this period, but career and financial responsibility are secondary.

CHALLENGES OF THE TRADITIONAL MODEL

The traditional model can work extremely well as long as both partners choose it and are satisfied with their roles. The model is simple, supported by tradition, and comes naturally to many individuals. However, traditional marriage can only flourish in a society that rewards the breadwinner with a stable salary that can adequately support a family and protects adults and children against economic misfortune. The society must also provide generously for the reentry to the workplace of the partner who stays home. Today, more and more cultures are fostering a business mentality that not only assumes the father—but increasingly the mother—will not make the family a priority, thus removing the traditional model as a viable option for the masses.

Low points in the traditional family most often occur with financial strain or when there is a transition—whether forced or voluntary—to another relationship model. So-called wifely duties taken for granted in the traditional marriage, such as housework and sex on demand, become negotiable when the woman is working outside the home just like the man. This is where flexibility separates the satisfied and dissatisfied relationships. Take the example of the Taylors.

Zach and Brendan talked about the pros and cons before they made the decision for her to take the Realtor's position she had recently been offered. Even though Zach was looking forward to the extra money Brendan would make, he was afraid that she would find it too stressful to work full-time. Brendan felt that since their only child, Craig, was in middle school, now was the time for her to go back to her chosen profession. Everything seemed to go fine the first few months, but gradually Brendan felt more and more discomfort. She was tired much of the time and felt resentful toward Zach, but she didn't mention it for a long time. She had been the one who wanted to go to work full-time, so she felt like she couldn't complain. Plus, she loved her job. Each morning she went to work with a positive attitude and her days went by like a flash. But as the time got closer to going home, her anxiety would start to build. By the time she walked in the door, there was a chip on her shoulder. Each time Brendan tried talking to Zach, it seemed like he just got defensive. By the time they came to me, they were in a real low spot.

Not long into our first session, Brendan expressed her frustration with Zach's lack of support. It didn't take him long to respond.

"Brendan, you were the one who wanted to go to work full-time. I told you it would be stressful, but you did it anyway."

"I know," she replied, "but I thought you would be more supportive."

"I have been supportive!" Zach emphasized. "What more do you want from me? You're the one who chose this."

"You just don't care," Brendan sighed, looking out the window and going silent.

Zach looked at me for help. It seemed time for Brendan to take ownership by acknowledging specifically what she wanted and needed from him.

"What's one small thing Zach could do that would be supportive of you?" I asked kindly.

She continued to stare out the window silently, then she

looked at me and said, "Well, he could do more around the house."

"Take a moment and think of one small thing he could do around the house that would feel like support to you. Then tell him," I suggested.

She looked at him for a moment then said, "You could fix dinner once in a while."

Zach gasped, then blurted, "You threw me out of the kitchen years ago! You know that."

"I know, but it's different now," Brendan replied.

Zach looked frustrated. He sighed, crossed his arms, and looked out the window. After a period of silence, he turned to her.

"Well, I can do it, but I can't guarantee what it will taste like. Can't I just bring home takeout?" he asked.

"How about you cook hamburgers one night and then bring takeout another night?" Brendan chirped.

"You're pushing your luck," Zach laughed.

This couple made it through this transition with a little help from me, but they could have done it themselves had they gathered information and clarified their roles to reflect current needs. When they originally discussed the change, they had failed to acknowledge the concept of equity, which is an essential part of true love. Being equitable means striving for overall fairness, that is, being fair about your expectations in the relationship. Attempting to achieve equity in a relationship is much more realistic and manageable than attempting to be equal all the time. Brendan didn't demand that Zach cook 3.5 meals per week, but that he pitch in and help at least once a week to lighten her load. People who advocate for 50-50 are often trapped in the process of keeping score, always making sure not to give more than they get. This is exhausting, unrealistic, and also very unsatisfying. At any given time a relationship will likely favor one person more than the other. The important question is: over time does it even out?

THE REVERSE TRADITIONAL MODEL— A 180 DEGREE TURN

Today, 30 percent of working wives of all ages—from their twenties to their sixties—are paid more than their husbands. Many of these marriages follow the reverse traditional model, with the female as the primary breadwinner and the male taking more of a supportive role to accommodate the demands of her higher paying job. The reality of time makes it hard to support two demanding jobs, so many couples choose to make the job with the higher earning potential the priority, and more and more often this job belongs to the woman. Sometimes couples intentionally choose the reverse traditional model; other times it is simply a result of job opportunities.

"I'VE BECOME THE MAN MY MOTHER ALWAYS WANTED ME TO MARRY"

Isabella and David intended to have a traditional marriage as soon as their first child was born. Having married after they were each past age thirty, their plan was for both of them to work for three years, then begin their family and Isabella become a stay-at-home mom. However, at the end of the second year, the start-up company where Isabella had been employed for almost ten years was sold, and in the reorganization, she was offered a management position with a large salary increase and stock options. By the time the three years rolled around, her salary had doubled, she was in line for an executive vice president's position—and she was pregnant. With the baby's arrival only weeks away, she and David were faced with a serious dilemma. Isabella had been assured that she had a good chance to be placed in the VP job, which would mean a much higher salary, a significant bonus, plus more stock. But this wasn't the biggest carrot. It was widely rumored that the company was going public. If she got the VP position and the additional stock and then the company went public, she and David could become very wealthy overnight.

After careful consideration and much discussion, they decided to go ahead with their plan but with a slight alteration. They decided that when the baby was born, David would become a stay-at-home dad. They would have the traditional family—only in reverse.

Their plan worked far better than they ever believed. David found that he not only loved being a full-time parent, he also had a strong domestic talent. Isabella did get the promotion and even before the company went public (it eventually did), they hired a housekeeper two days a week to make everyone's role easier. Exercising flexibility, David became a full-time homemaker while Isabella continued to be the financial provider. Even though this model felt equitable and worked well for them and their relationship, from time to time they still had to face disapproval from some family members and friends.

Although traditional male and female roles have changed, perceptions have not caught up. Even in the new millennium, a man in the role of homemaker can still pose a threat to traditional masculinity. His so-called worth as a man may be called into question. For centuries women have fought the notion that their job as homemaker is less important than the man's job as provider. In the reverse traditional model, men often find this same lack of respect.

The economic changes of the past century have impacted the family in a powerful way, and all indications are that we are going to see even more changes. In a current list of Fortune 500 top female executives, six of the ten had stay-at-home husbands. With more women receiving college degrees than men, it is likely that they will continue to become the higher wage earner—and a greater number of men will become more involved with children, home, and nurturing. Regardless of which partner takes on the primary duties of wage earner or support person, it is important that each maintain skills that will make him/her a productive member of the outside workforce. Such hardships as divorce, illness, death, layoffs, and economic bust loom as catastrophes that could force an unplanned reversal of roles. A safety net of earning potential for both partners is advisable, because the truth about roles in today's relationships is—they are ever changing.

"FOR BETTER, FOR WORSE, BUT NOT FOR LUNCH!"

Many couples switch from the traditional to the reverse traditional model at midlife. The traditional man shifts his focus from work to family and/or outside activities. The woman, who has stayed home with the children and/or supported her husband's career, begins to look at her options, which often include working outside the home.

Two of our closest friends, Burt and Gelene Johnson, have switched roles many times during the forty years they've been together. They began married life working on a large farm in Minnesota that had been in Burt's family for over a century. For their first twenty years, Burt provided for the family through the efforts of the farm. Gelene supported him in every way she could while raising ten children (eight biological, two adopted). Once the children were old enough to help one another, Gelene returned to school to get her master's degree in music pedagogy while Burt continued to farm.

Gelene finished her degree just as the big farming crisis began to take shape. Thousands of farmers lost their land. Fortunately, the Johnsons had seen this change coming and were prepared for Gelene to step in and provide financial support while Burt "retired." At this time they switched roles completely. She opened her own music school with Burt assisting in every way, from building the studio to holding down the domestic front. He learned to cook, clean, and do laundry. At the same time, he took care of all the pets, the yard, and graciously entertained friends. I can remember twenty years ago when you would go to their house for dinner and Gelene would be working feverishly putting the meal on the table. Now when you arrive, she gets to chat while Burt performs his magic as the gourmet. Recently they made another shift in their roles. Burt took a full-time job as clerk of the water board in their community. Gelene is making plans for an earlier retirement. I wonder how many couples could have managed the transitions this couple has mastered.

Today, marriage has to allow for greater flexibility. If two people begin their marriage with a mind toward equity and changing roles, they stand a much greater chance of success. Now let's take a look at the most common model of relationship couples are using today.

THE NEO-TRADITIONAL MODEL

The vast majority of couples today live neither in the traditional or the reverse traditional model of marriage. Instead, they live in a model which features two people working outside the home, with the after-work responsibilities divided in sundry ways. I call this the neo-traditional model. This model has been referred to as the two-income or dual-career couple, but that doesn't say enough. A better term might be the stressed-to-the-limits or meeting-myself-coming-and-going couple.

Couples with partners who both work outside the home are part of the first generation experiencing "life without a wife." The biggest problem with this model is that all those "wifely tasks" are still waiting for you when you walk in the door each evening! If the work at home is divided along traditional gender lines, this means the woman will basically have two full-time jobs.

When both people work outside the home, what waits at the

door to be done at the end of the day is more than one person can manage—and still have any quality of life. The biggest problem in the neo-traditional marriage is exhaustion brought on by over-work and stress.

Equitable couples in the neo-traditional model divide tasks along lines of preference, convenience, availability, or ability. They take turns, focus on priorities, hire what they can afford done, enlist the help of children, barter—you name it. They also become experts at taking shortcuts whenever possible. (When I was a full-time homemaker I cooked almost every meal. Now when I tell my kids it's time to eat, they go get in the car!)

THE GOOD NEWS

The benefits of the neo-traditional model are many, including greater personal freedom, more choices, and increased control over one's life. Each person is respected as being capable of han-dling the many tasks of home, as well as the workplace. The neo-traditional structure gives children role models that are not confined by gender, which enables them to have more freedom to follow their own interests. Children have access to two parents instead of one, since parenting is more of a joint than individual role. This model holds unlimited variety, and can help avoid one of the greatest enemies of relationships—boredom. Although it takes a great deal of energy, it is rarely ever dull. But because of its complexity and ever changing nature, the neo-traditional model requires organization, trust, awareness, and maturity. When you live in a world with no foregone conclusions, no role models, and everything open to discussion, you need two com-mitted people who can take the frequent highs and lows in stride.

When Kim and Walter married, she was a schoolteacher and he was the district manager for a pharmaceutical company. Their first two years were much like any marriage. They were busy with the tasks of establishing a home, getting to know relatives, and

generally settling into married life. During the third year they
had their first child, Sammy, and shortly after Kim returned to
work, she accepted a position as head of curriculum development
to allow for a more flexible work schedule. When Sammy was
three, Kim was offered a statewide curriculum position, which
would require about six days of travel each month. She was excited about the offer and the career challenge it presented; however, when she opened the discussion with Walter, she was met
with a great deal of resistance.

He was very uncomfortable with the idea of her traveling,
mainly because his job also required travel days. He wanted Kim
to stay in her present position and continue to be the primary
parent for Sammy. At first, Kim saw Walter's point of view as selfish and sexist, but after several lengthy discussions they asked
themselves the question: "What is best for our family and our relationship?"

The answer was clear to both of them: for Kim to stay in her
present position. Once she looked at the proposed change from
this perspective, the decision was made. Although she was disappointed, she did not feel resentful. Ironically, about six months after this decision, Walter had an opportunity to change jobs. The
new position offered more money and about the same travel, but
he would have to drive twenty minutes further each way to work.
When they began discussing the offer, at first Kim felt resentful
that he was considering changing jobs when she had made the decision not to. But once she asked herself "What is best for the family and the relationship?" she knew that the extra money would
help them and relieve some stress. Her flexible hours made the
added time Walter would be away from home negligible.

The neo-traditional couple has to grapple with important issues that are predetermined in the traditional model. For example, if both individuals work outside the home, whose job will
take priority? What if one person is happy in his/her job and the

other gets a great job opportunity requiring a move? Will all income be combined? Will there be joint or individual checking accounts? What will be the rules about personal spending? How will major financial decisions be made? Will debt be acquired jointly, individually, or both? What will debt limitations be? Who decides when you will have sex? Do you have sex when you don't want to? And what about raising children? Who will be the primary parent? Who will stay home when Johnny is sick? There is the issue of household chores. Who will do the job nobody wants? And who will have the final say when there are disagreements?

Most of us have to unlearn old habits to effectively create a neo-traditional relationship. People who take on this challenge frequently find that they have a foot in both worlds and still hold unrealistic expectations that are left over from the traditional model. For example, a woman who works full-time may still expect the house to look like there is a full-time homemaker cleaning every day. Or the man who comes home from work might expect to have the whole evening to relax while his wife takes on the household tasks. Or the couple who both work sixty hours a week expect to have energy left over for home and family. What are your unrealistic expectations about the roles in relationship?

CLARIFYING YOUR MODEL

I am not making a case for one of these models being better than the other. The important point is: you both need to be living realistically—and working from the same script. Most often problems arise when partners have different expectations. Cindie, a woman I met on a cruise ship, was celebrating what would have been her fifteenth wedding anniversary—but without her husband. Here's the way she explained their conflict. "I should have known our marriage would never make it when my ex-husband chose 'Wind Beneath My Wings' as our wedding song. Problem was: we could never decide who was the wind and who was the wings." They had each expected to be the primary breadwinner with the full support of the other partner. They never came to an agreement and eventually their conflict wore them down and destroyed the marriage.

CLARIFYING YOUR ROLE PREFERENCES AND EXPECTATIONS IS IMPORTANT IN A SATISFYING RELATIONSHIP

Take a moment to explore your thoughts about roles by answering these questions:

Are you and your partner in agreement about the model your relationship follows?

Look at the conflicts that come up between you and your partner. Are any of these related to your roles within the relationship?

Which model best describes the model of relationship you and your partner are using? Have you talked openly about this?

If you had your first choice, which model would you honestly prefer?

What is it that appeals to you about this model?

What issues come up because you prefer this model?

What are the disadvantages of this model?

Which model does your partner prefer?

Are there any difficulties as a result of his or her preference?

Is your relationship equitable? Does it feel fair?

Do you feel supported in your relationship?

Do you fulfill your partner's expectations in this relationship?

What, if any, changes need to be made in the model of relationship you are using?

Is there flexibility and room for discussion about changing the model and/or roles you are using?

Are there any immediate issues the two of you need to address related to current roles within the relationship? If so, what are they?

MIXED MESSAGES

Sometimes individuals set themselves up for a low spot in relationships by sending their partner mixed messages about roles. A man might appreciate the financial benefits of his career-oriented partner but be resentful when her career outshines his. A woman might say she wants a gentle, sensitive, emotionally vulnerable man but expect this same guy to compete and win in the cutthroat business world.

GROWING PAINS

As women and men begin to experiment with the neo-traditional model, the transition will naturally have some rough spots. For example, when men co-parent, women have to face the loss of privilege that goes with being the primary parent. If mom has been the one who can "kiss a boo-boo and make it better," with the advent of co-parenting she has to be willing to share this special role. Women must also be willing to respect a parenting style other than their own. Many women say they want collaborative parenting, but then they step in to "correct" the father when he doesn't follow their model. Men also have some stretching to do in their role of the support person. For instance, they may have to become the spouse on the arm at office parties or the one who watches the kids while mom goes to the "good old boy happy hour."

Obviously, the transition from the traditional model has not been an easy one, and divorce rates reflect the difficulty. But changing and clarifying roles does not have to threaten your relationship; in fact, it can revitalize it. Here are some tips:

- Keep in mind that love is a response to getting your needs met, so do what works for the two of you.

- Understand that roles change and need frequent negotiation, even renegotiation.

- Get your expectations in line with reality. If you both work outside the home—unless you have a full-time housekeeper—expectations need to adjust accordingly.

- Flexibility is the key in any model.

- Prioritizing is imperative. One guideline I learned years ago is, "Some things you can only do once in life—others you can do anytime." A child is only a child once—graduate school for you is always there. Birthdays come once a year—the house needs cleaning all year long.

- Make sure you are in agreement about the model for your relationship. Frequent arguments and dissatisfaction are often the result of differing expectations and working at cross-purposes.

- Expect change.

- Expect transitions to take more time and attention than you planned. However, rest assured that each transition you address together can deepen your love and satisfaction.

As roles change, couples need a road map to guide them through the low spots as each partner continues to broaden his/her talents and options. Couples need to reapply the lessons of discovery as they balance work, family commitments, housework, economic power, personal time, and interests. Clarifying roles can give you clear guidelines for making your relationship run smoothly. The next discovery chapter, "Defining Love," will tell you how to make your relationship exciting.

5

Discovery: Defining Love

During the past ten years, I have been very fortunate to be involved in many talk shows and interviews. On more than one occasion, with less than thirty seconds left on the air, I have been asked, "Dr. Love, tell us: how can we create satisfying love that will last a lifetime?" About the second or third time I was asked that question, I came up with an answer that gets to the bottom line. The truth about creating love that will last a lifetime is: find out what says "I love you" to your partner, and then do it! It works every time.

But in order to follow that simple direction, you first have to discover what touches your partner's heart. Here are some guidelines for doing this.

THE THREE Cs

In the Western culture we expect long-term love to contain some combination of chemistry, compatibility, and commitment. Chemistry is the force that gets you together with a genetic match and provides sexual excitement and romance. Compatibility sustains the relationship over the years and sweetens your daily life through cooperative companionship. The role of commitment is to provide a sense of permanence and security. Although most of us want all of these ingredients, each individual has specific preferences, as well as priorities. Some actions touch your heart more than others. Happy, mature couples continue to discover and rediscover each other's priorities and organize their relationship accordingly. This next exercise is designed to help you come up with your own unique definition of love.

DEFINING LOVE

Rank the following items in terms of how important they are to you in a relationship. Rank them on a scale from 1 to 6, with 1 being "not important," 6 being "very important."

1. Physical affection.
   Not Important   Somewhat Important   Very Important
      1   2   3   4   5   6

2. Sexual touching.
   Not Important   Somewhat Important   Very Important
      1   2   3   4   5   6

3. Having sex.
   Not Important   Somewhat Important   Very Important
      1   2   3   4   5   6

4. Being excited about sex.
   Not Important   Somewhat Important   Very Important
      1   2   3   4   5   6

5. Pleasing one another sexually.
   Not Important   Somewhat Important   Very Important
      1   2   3   4   5   6

6. Keeping romance alive with gifts, cards, gestures.
   Not Important   Somewhat Important   Very Important
      1   2   3   4   5   6

7. Having fun with my partner.
   Not Important   Somewhat Important   Very Important
      1   2   3   4   5   6

8. Getting along well on a regular basis.
   Not Important   Somewhat Important   Very Important
      1   2   3   4   5   6

9. Being able to share my feelings with my partner.

Not Important		Somewhat Important		Very Important	
1	2	3	4	5	6

10. Being able to talk openly with my partner.

Not Important		Somewhat Important		Very Important	
1	2	3	4	5	6

11. Having my partner support me.

Not Important		Somewhat Important		Very Important	
1	2	3	4	5	6

12. Putting effort and energy into the relationship.

Not Important		Somewhat Important		Very Important	
1	2	3	4	5	6

13. Trusting my partner to be faithful.

Not Important		Somewhat Important		Very Important	
1	2	3	4	5	6

14. Having my partner be honest with me.

Not Important		Somewhat Important		Very Important	
1	2	3	4	5	6

15. Getting financial support from my partner.

Not Important		Somewhat Important		Very Important	
1	2	3	4	5	6

16. Getting a permanent commitment.

Not Important		Somewhat Important		Very Important	
1	2	3	4	5	6

17. Spending time as a couple with friends.

Not Important		Somewhat Important		Very Important	
1	2	3	4	5	6

18. Spending time as a couple with family.

Not Important		Somewhat Important		Very Important	
1	2	3	4	5	6

Once you have answered each question, first add the total scores for items 1 through 6, which relate to chemistry.
Place your score for the chemistry items here:_____

Now, add your total scores for items 7 through 12, which relate to compatibility. Place your score for the compatibility items here:_____

Finally, add your total scores for items 13 through 18, which relate to commitment. Place your commitment score here:_____

Once you have scores for each category, look at the columns below and circle the range that contains your score for each category.

Chemistry	Compatibility	Commitment	Range
31–36	31–36	31–36	High
25–30	25–30	25–30	High
19–24	19–24	19–24	Moderate
13–18	13–18	13–18	Moderate
7–12	7–12	7–12	Low
1–6	1–6	1–6	Low

What insight can you gain from your scores?

Based upon your scores, how can a partner best show you love?

Would your partner answer differently?

How can you best show your partner love?

To understand how different couples define their love, let's take a look at some profiles.

THE HIGH-CHEMISTRY COUPLE

Couples in which both individuals rank sex and romance as the highest priority in their relationship have a lot of energy between them and feel just as much in love today as they did when they first met. If anything, their physical and sexual attraction has likely increased over time. This couple places a strong emphasis on great sex and uses the act of lovemaking to keep their relationship close. Their life together is one long extended courtship with lots of flirting, teasing, and sexual energy. The high-chemistry couple always feel in love, and in many ways their relationship represents what many of us expect "happily ever after" to look like.

Kenneta and Bill have been married for twenty-seven years and yet you would think they were newlyweds. When Bill comes into the room, Kenneta's eyes light up and she flirts with him unmercifully. Bill says he can be at work cutting grass at the golf course and be flooded with desire for her.

Arnie and Merilee were still having great sex right up until six months before he died at age seventy-three. Eight years later, Merilee still misses the sensual and sexual contact they had and is very open to finding a new partner and/or lover.

Obviously, this model works best for two people who really like sex and for whom it is a personal, as well as relational, priority—like in the examples mentioned above. The liability of this model is that a couple's sex life is the most vulnerable part of their marriage. Sex drive can be low for any number of reasons, including lack of intimate contact, childbirth, stress, and hormone levels, and these are the dangerous points for the high-chemistry couple.

THE OXYTOCIN CONNECTION

There is another reason the high-chemistry couple feels so much in love: sex deepens the love bond. This is a reason to have sex with your partner even if it takes effort to become aroused. As I talked about in the post-rapture chapter, when you engage in sex, your body releases the peptide oxytocin. This powerful neuro-transmitter has a profound effect on women, as well as men, by promoting bonding. Oxytocin is largely responsible for why you feel closer to your partner and more "in love" when you have reg- ular sex.

Here's how it works. Oxytocin sensitizes the skin to touch and encourages affectionate behavior. Oxytocin levels rise during subsequent touching and, once a pattern has been established, can increase with the mere anticipation of touching. The more affec-tionate you are, the more endorphins are released, which cause you to feel relaxed, tranquil, and more sexually receptive. Oxy-tocin increases again during sexual activity, spikes during orgasm, and remains elevated for a time afterward, flooding the two of you in the bond of love. It can even strengthen an erection and in-tensify ejaculation. Oxytocin also has an amnesic effect, in that it blocks memory. Its release during coitus and orgasm allows all that is negative to be forgiven—or at least forgotten for a period of time. Scientists believe this side effect evolved because it was useful as a survival mechanism. Oxytocin is also released during childbirth, helping to eradicate the memory of labor pain, and is activated again during nursing, helping the new mother bond to the baby and perhaps forget those sleepless nights.

Take the following quiz to see how important chemistry is to you in a relationship.

RATE YOUR CHEMISTRY

Rate each item by circling the number that represents how im-portant it is to you personally.

1. Making love frequently.

   Not Important   Somewhat Important   Very Important
      1   2   3   4   5   6

2. Having both of us excited about sex.

Not Important		Somewhat Important		Very Important	
1	2	3	4	5	6

3. Varying our lovemaking.

Not Important		Somewhat Important		Very Important	
1	2	3	4	5	6

4. Being physically desired by my partner.

Not Important		Somewhat Important		Very Important	
1	2	3	4	5	6

5. Having strong physical desire for my partner.

Not Important		Somewhat Important		Very Important	
1	2	3	4	5	6

6. Helping each other keep our desire level high.

Not Important		Somewhat Important		Very Important	
1	2	3	4	5	6

7. Meeting each other's sexual needs.

Not Important		Somewhat Important		Very Important	
1	2	3	4	5	6

8. Being romantic with each other.

Not Important		Somewhat Important		Very Important	
1	2	3	4	5	6

9. Having regular "dates."

Not Important		Somewhat Important		Very Important	
1	2	3	4	5	6

10 . Keeping our lovemaking fresh and exciting.

Not Important		Somewhat Important		Very Important	
1	2	3	4	5	6

Total possible points: 60

Your total score: _____

Based on your score, plus what you know about yourself, how important is chemistry (i.e., physical attraction, sex, and romance) to you in your relationship? Place an X on the line below to indicate.

_____

Not Important   Somewhat Important   Very Important

Now, place an O to indicate how important the role of chemistry is to your partner.

Finally, place an R to indicate how important you think chemistry is to your relationship.

QUESTIONS TO PONDER:

What role would you like chemistry to play in your relationship?

What would you like from your partner in terms of sex, romance, and/or physical attraction? How could you increase the likelihood this will happen?

How could you improve your role as a sex/romantic partner?

WHAT IF I'M IN A "MIXED-CHEMISTRY MARRIAGE"?
It is not uncommon for one partner to have a greater interest in sex and romance than the other; therefore, it is important for you to come to a satisfying agreement that incorporates your differences. Here are some tips.

If you are the high-chemistry (also likely the high-testosterone) person:

Let your partner know about your desire and what sex is like for you.

Often the person with the higher desire assumes the partner is aware of the strong desire he/she has for sexual contact, and the discomfort and frustration that occurs when you go without sex. Believing this, there is little choice but to feel punished, hurt, or at least confused when needs are seemingly ignored. However, the low-T person does not experience this same discomfort without frequent sex. Unless the high-T person is clear about the seriousness of the situation, the low-T partner will never know. This is when ownership is very important. Let your needs be known. Ask for what you want in a loving, respectful way.

Make sure you express desire for your partner, but not just for sex. At times you might need to be specific: "I want to make love to you." "I'm hot for your body." "You turn me on." "I really want to touch you." "I love the way you make me feel."

Understand that your partner can get a great deal of pleasure from giving you pleasure, and that may be all she/he wants or needs at the time. When I was conducting the research for the book *Hot Monogamy* that I coauthored with Jo Robinson, I took a healthy dose of testosterone under a doctor's supervision. Let me tell you, it is very different having a strong sex drive! While I was on that drug I thought about sex. I fantasized about sex. I wanted sex. Sexual thoughts came into my mind uninvited. I made sexual innuendoes. I looked at men sexually. I admired their butts, I looked at their crotch, and without frequent sex, I became irritable. I don't think any research study, any interview, or any book could have convinced this normally low-T person what it was like to be a high-T. It was a real eye-opener, and it humbled me appropriately. Before I had that experience, it was easy for me to be insensitive to my partner's needs, but afterward I understood what it was like lying on the other side of the bed.

If you are a low-chemistry person paired with a high-chemistry partner:

Be proactive about your arousal. First of all, you might want to check out physical causes related to low libido. Find a medical person who will work with you and take your desire level seriously. For women, there are many ways to enhance your libido, from diet and exercise to hormone replacement therapy. Your gynecologist may be the person to talk with first. For men, a urologist may provide the most assistance. Your physician should be familiar with the wide range of treatment options, which guarantee most any man an erection.

The good news is: you can decide what kind of lover you want to be and take steps to create this person. You begin by first clarifying your sexual goals. How often do you want to be sexual, what form would you like the sex play to take, what type of stimulation do you need, and how do you want to respond? Become clear about your own needs and desires, and then be willing to share these with your partner.

Make room in your life for sex. Again, you will likely need to be proactive and make plans for it. Rituals are great for setting aside time for making love, such as taking a hot bath before you go to bed, even going to bed earlier to save energy for sex, or initiating sex in the morning when you are fresh and more energized. If you have young children, find another couple who will trade baby-sitting with you on a regular basis to allow time for a romantic evening.

Become an expert on your own arousal. Find out what turns you on. Some of us have to jump-start our libido and cannot expect another person to know more than we do. Explore the options. Read books, watch tapes, talk to others, get advice, and stimulate yourself. Also, pay attention to subtle cues. If you have even a hint of sexual energy, take advantage of it, make an overture, fan the flames of desire, and run with it. Don't sit around waiting for an erotic earthquake. Be happy with a tremor.

Be clear, kind, and direct about your sexual needs. If you need different foreplay, more time together, more help around the house, kinder words, a more gentle touch—say it. Give information at a time when your relationship is in a good place, and when you are not having sex. Also, feel free to use more than words to teach your partner. Gently guide your partner's hand to the spot that feels best. Reinforce the techniques that please you with soft sounds like "umm." Let your partner know what he or she is doing right. Nothing succeeds like success. We all want to feel like we are good lovers.

Be sensitive and realistic about your partner's sexual needs. You may not want sex very often or even desire to be sexual; however, that may not be the case for your partner. Look at what it is like living with you. Imagine having a high sex drive and having you as a partner. What would that be like? What would be best for your relationship?

Since you will likely be the one who determines how much sex the two of you have, when you say no to sex, say what you are willing to do or when you will be available for sex. "I'd be glad to give you a backrub." Or, "Tonight doesn't work for me; however, tomorrow night, you are mine!" Again, it might help to imagine what it would be like to have a burning desire for sex and be turned down flat with no indication of when your need will be met and no offer of affection or kindness.

THE HIGH-COMPATIBILITY COUPLE

What a pleasure it is to be in the company of two people who get along well, and how unpleasant it is to be with those who don't! For decades studies have shown that satisfied couples fill their days with kindness and respect, greatly outweighing negative interactions with positives. Many of these same couples say that compatibility and friendship are keys to their success. Companionship and shared interests bond these two, who often begin their relationship as friends and evolve into lovers. High-compatibility couples get along very well and find that they confide and consult with one another on a regular basis. It is not uncommon for this couple to talk to each other several times a day even when one or both are at work. They spend a great deal of time together in the roles of confidant and playmate, financial, social, and domestic partners. They look and act like best friends.

Take a look at the following exercises to get a reading on how important compatibility is to you in your relationship.

HOW IMPORTANT IS COMPATIBILITY TO YOU?

If you truly value compatibility in your relationship, it will be reflected in your behavior; otherwise, it may be an ideal instead of a value. Simply answer true (T) or false (F) to the following questions to determine how important compatibility is to you.

1. _____ My partner would say I am easy to get along with.

2. _____ I manage my temperament to fit well with my partner.

3. _____ My style of communicating makes me easy to live with.

4. _____ I am fun to be with.

5. _____ In the past my partner's requests have resulted in changes in my behavior.

6. _____ My partner and I have mutual interests.

7. _____ My partner would say I am easy to work with.

8. _____ When things aren't going well between us, I make sure we get back on track.

9. _____ I carry my weight in our relationship.

10. _____ My behavior shows a strong sense of fairness.

11. _____ My partner and I enjoy spending time together.

12. _____ My partner knows me very well.

13. _____ I make it a point to give my partner information.

14._____I show active interest in my partner's life.

15._____My partner is my best friend.

16._____My partner knows me better than anyone else.

Total true answers out of a possible 16:_____

HOW COMPATIBLE ARE YOU AND YOUR PARTNER?

Indicate how compatible you and your partner are in the areas lised below by using the following scale:

Not Compatible		Somewhat Compatible		Very Compatible	
1	2	3	4	5	6

1. Money

Not Compatible		Somewhat Compatible		Very Compatible	
1	2	3	4	5	6

2. Being on time

Not Compatible		Somewhat Compatible		Very Compatible	
1	2	3	4	5	6

3. Preferences in food

Not Compatible		Somewhat Compatible		Very Compatible	
1	2	3	4	5	6

4. Preferences for friends

Not Compatible		Somewhat Compatible		Very Compatible	
1	2	3	4	5	6

5. Amount of time spent together

Not Compatible		Somewhat Compatible		Very Compatible	
1	2	3	4	5	6

6. Entertainment

Not Compatible		Somewhat Compatible		Very Compatible	
1	2	3	4	5	6

7. Music preferences
    <u>Not Compatible</u>   <u>Somewhat Compatible</u>   <u>Very Compatible</u>
      1   2   3   4   5   6

8. Spending time with family
    <u>Not Compatible</u>   <u>Somewhat Compatible</u>   <u>Very Compatible</u>
      1   2   3   4   5   6

9. How clean the house should be
    <u>Not Compatible</u>   <u>Somewhat Compatible</u>   <u>Very Compatible</u>
      1   2   3   4   5   6

10. Pets
    <u>Not Compatible</u>   <u>Somewhat Compatible</u>   <u>Very Compatible</u>
      1   2   3   4   5   6

11. Alcohol
    <u>Not Compatible</u>   <u>Somewhat Compatible</u>   <u>Very Compatible</u>
      1   2   3   4   5   6

12. Religion or spirituality
    <u>Not Compatible</u>   <u>Somewhat Compatible</u>   <u>Very Compatible</u>
      1   2   3   4   5   6

13. Job or career
    <u>Not Compatible</u>   <u>Somewhat Compatible</u>   <u>Very Compatible</u>
      1   2   3   4   5   6

14. Leisure time activities
    <u>Not Compatible</u>   <u>Somewhat Compatible</u>   <u>Very Compatible</u>
      1   2   3   4   5   6

15. Sex
    <u>Not Compatible</u>   <u>Somewhat Compatible</u>   <u>Very Compatible</u>
      1   2   3   4   5   6

16. Intimate talking
    <u>Not Compatible</u>   <u>Somewhat Compatible</u>   <u>Very Compatible</u>
      1   2   3   4   5   6

Other_____

Not Compatible		Somewhat Compatible		Very Compatible	
1	2	3	4	5	6

What are your thoughts about your scores in the exercises above?

How could you improve the compatibility in your relationship?

What area(s) do you need to address in order for your relationship to be even more compatible?

COMPATIBILITY CAUTION

One of the ironic liabilities of the high-compatibility couple is that it can get too comfortable. Since they get along so well, it's often easier to do things together than to include others. The couple's friendship can take priority to the detriment of other relationships and result in isolation and exclusion. This takes away an important source of energy and puts the relationship at risk for boredom. Also, the high-compatibility couple can lapse into a friendly brother-sister relationship that lacks any form of passion. That's fine if both are comfortable with this; however, if one or both want sexual excitement, this couple will likely have to work at it. And since there is such a cultural emphasis placed on sex and romantic love in relationships, unless you nurture the chemistry, one or both partners may fall into the fallacious "I love you but I'm not in love with you" syndrome mentioned earlier. Therefore, high-compatibility couples are well advised to push the envelope in the sexual area from time to time. This means stepping out of the role of best friends into the lover category with one another.

COMPATIBILITY IS THE LIFEBLOOD OF TRUE LOVE

Last summer, I had the privilege of attending a presentation of my friend and colleague Michelle Weiner-Davis, author of the best-selling book *Divorce Busting*. I have known Michelle for several years and I learn something from her every time I hear her speak. This particular occasion, her words held special wisdom. Basically, she said that one of the reasons many people are not happy in a relationship is that they would rather be right than happy. When people become so invested in the logic of their opinion, they lose sight of the fact that the overall goal is to be close and connected.

Dr. Weiner-Davis's insight poses important questions: Does your behavior reflect your desire to be more compatible with your partner? Do you show the same respect in your manner, tone of voice, and attitude that you do for others you value and hold in esteem? Do you treat your partner with the same kindness you would show another good friend? Do you make time for mutually enjoyable activities with your partner? Do you initiate these activities? Do you laugh a lot with your partner? Do you create humorous interactions between you? Have you orchestrated fun activities for the two of you? And finally, what can be learned from other friendships that can increase compatibility with your partner?

Without a doubt compatibility is the lifeblood of true love. Research and common sense alike tell us that being kind, caring, friendly, positive, good-natured, apologetic, and well mannered in your relationship is the best investment in home improvement.

THE HIGH-COMMITMENT COUPLE

High-commitment couples value being in a partnership and enjoy the lifestyle that comes with living with someone on a permanent basis. These individuals take pleasure in having a spouse and much prefer partnership to being alone. Those who highly value commitment often relate to their extended families and the broader community as a unit. They like to be seen as a couple and like to be known as committed. High-commitment couples often have children and see child care as one of the most important functions of their relationship. When high-chemistry or high-compatibility couples have children, their relationship satisfaction goes down for a while. But when high-commitment couples have children, their marital satisfaction goes up because children are seen as an integral part of their relationship. This couple is often very family-oriented and plan most of their activities to include other people.

TYPES OF COMMITMENT

On the surface it might appear that commitment is a basic concept and everyone would rate it high in terms of defining love. However, there are different types of commitment. One form of commitment is to the marriage or staying together "for better, for worse, in sickness and in health, till death do us part." In this type, individuals are committed to each other, regardless of the relationship quality. Another form of commitment is to the relationship and making it better. The high-commitment couple commits to the relationship as well as staying together, pledging to do what it takes to keep the union vibrant and satisfying. This is not necessarily the case for other couples.

"WHAT DO YOU MEAN I DON'T LOVE YOU—I MARRIED YOU, DIDN'T I?"

Lucas was quite the romantic during the two years he was courting Mackenzie. But shortly after their wedding, it became evident that marriage had been his ultimate goal. His primary desire was to have someone at home when he came in from work or spending time with his buddies. He had little interest in developing a deep friendship with his wife and was only moderately interested in their sex life. Lucas was uneasy, even annoyed, with Mackenzie's desire for more personal conversations and fully expected her to save those needs for her female friends. Despite these facts, he loved his wife and was committed to her. He was a faithful husband and a responsible provider, and he wanted to have children.

Lucas was committed to the institution or idea of marriage, but he wasn't committed to the relationship; therefore, we could not call them a high-commitment couple. The quality of their sex life was not strong, their friendship was lacking, and their commitment was only partial. The prognosis for satisfaction in this relationship would not be good unless Mackenzie shared his preference, which she did not. This couple came to me after she had left him. Even though her leaving served as a serious wake-up call and he discovered far more commitment to the relationship than he thought he had, it took several months to repair the hurt and disappointment that his lack of commitment to the relationship had caused.

"MIGHT AS WELL FACE IT, I'M COMMITTED TO LOVE"

Sometimes people don't commit to marriage or to the relationship but simply to love. They fall in love and remain committed as long as love lasts. When love lags, they leave. One of the obvious hazards of this type of "commitment lite" is that love has normal ups and downs, changing like the seasons. Sometimes it's hot; sometimes it's cool. Occasionally you have a long serious drought. Without commitment to more than just love, you can mistake a season of little love for the end of love—and give up a perfectly suitable relationship.

"DEVOTED TO YOU"

Another type of commitment is to the person. You fall in love and commit to the individual. There is an obvious pitfall to this approach—people change. Say you fall in love with someone because you are awed by his or her knowledge. That's fine as long as you don't know much, but what happens when you become just as knowledgeable? Or, say you fall in love with a gorgeous body.

What happens when that body has cellulite and love handles? Countless times in my work with couples I have heard "you weren't that way when I married you." All we have to do is look at old photos to see that change is inevitable for all of us. Plus, infatuation gives us such an idealized image of our partner that no one could live up to it. Disappointment is inevitable, and handling it is a part of maturity.

SO WHAT ARE YOU COMMITTING TO?

Commitment gives you the right to expect your partner to meet at least some of your needs some of the time. It doesn't mean you get all of your needs met all of the time; it's simply a promise of some type of availability. This is often why people won't commit. They don't want the other person to have the right to expect something they don't want to do. In satisfying marriages, the roles are clear concerning commitment and what each partner has the right to expect from the other.

Unlike the scenarios just mentioned here, the high-commitment couple has made a promise to do whatever it takes to create a satisfying relationship. These individuals have a sense of "we-ness." They think of themselves as individuals, as well as part of a unit. They give close attention not only to their own happiness but also to the well-being of the relationship.

One has to be committed to the relationship to ensure long-term satisfaction and survive the highs and lows of love. When love is going through a normal lull, you do what is best for the relationship even if you may not be inclined to do what is best for your partner. Doing what you think is best for you might not be best for the relationship. None of us is perfect enough to merit undying devotion on a daily basis. There has to be a commitment to something bigger. Commitment to the marriage takes over where commitment to the person ends. Commitment to the relationship transcends the highs and lows of love. Take a look at the following exercise to see what role commitment plays in your relationship.

HOW COMMITTED ARE YOU TO THE RELATIONSHIP?

Read the following statements and circle the number that best represents your response.

1. I am committed to doing whatever it takes to make this relationship work.

   <u>Disagree</u>   <u>Somewhat Agree</u>   <u>Strongly Agree</u>
     1   2   3   4   5   6

2. I think I could do more to improve our relationship.

   <u>Disagree</u>   <u>Somewhat Agree</u>   <u>Strongly Agree</u>
     1   2   3   4   5   6

3. Commitment is a source of satisfaction in our relationship.

   <u>Disagree</u>   <u>Somewhat Agree</u>   <u>Strongly Agree</u>
     1   2   3   4   5   6

4. I am willing to put the needs of the relationship before my own needs.

   <u>Disagree</u>   <u>Somewhat Agree</u>   <u>Strongly Agree</u>
     1   2   3   4   5   6

5. I show appreciation to my partner for his/her commitment.

   <u>Disagree</u>   <u>Somewhat Agree</u>   <u>Strongly Agree</u>
     1   2   3   4   5   6

Total score _____ **out of a possible 30**

What would make your overall commitment rating higher?

What are your thoughts about your commitment at this point in time?

MIXED-PRIORITY MARRIAGES

Many couples have mixed priorities in marriage. Often a person who has chemistry (sex) as the highest priority in relationship will pair up with a partner who holds compatibility or friendship as the number one preference. Or someone who simply wants the security of commitment will fall in love with someone who wants more compatibility. While this adds diversity to the relationship, it can also be a source of conflict. Without skill and knowledge, these differences can greatly lower the satisfaction between you. Take a look at the following exercise. Let it help you determine the priorities and preferences that exist in your relationship, and give you suggestions for utilizing your differences.

DISCOVER YOUR PRIORITIES

Rank in order the three major roles in relationship—chemistry, compatibility, and commitment. Put 1 by your highest priority, 2 by your second, and 3 by your third.

Then, do your best to list your partner's priorities.

You   Your Partner

_____   _____   chemistry
_____   _____   compatibility
_____   _____   commitment

Look at the order of preferences for you and your partner. How can you make your relationship more satisfying based upon this information?

Look at your partner's number 1 preference. How well are you meeting his/her needs in this area? How could you improve?

List three creative ways that together you and your partner could meet one another's needs.

PROGRAM YOUR RELATIONSHIP FOR SATISFACTION

There are four guidelines for defining your expectations of love:

1. Be clear.
2. Be reasonable.
3. Be flexible.
4. Be equitable.

Being clear means communicating honestly with yourself, as well as your partner. It also includes specificity. Expressions such as "be thoughtful," "help around the house," "be intimate," "support me," "care for me," "be more romantic" are often too vague. Use language that is more precise: "I'd really like it if you supported me by coming to my office party next month on the 7th." Or, "I love it when you show your thoughtfulness by getting up with the children on Saturday morning and letting me sleep." Even "tell me what you did today" gives guidelines. Your partner can only satisfy you if he/she has a clear idea of what you want.

Being reasonable includes getting your expectations in line with reality. Unrealistic expectations are one of the biggest causes of dissatisfaction in marriage. Expecting your partner to have the same desires as you, to think the way you do, or to focus on your needs but not vice versa is unrealistic and will lead to dissatisfaction. Expecting your partner to meet all of your needs all of the time is another impractical expectation. In the conversation with Mary Lou at the wedding I mentioned in Chapter 3, she said living close to extended family had greatly helped her manage her needs and expectations. "When my husband wasn't interested in a particular subject, I could go visit my mother or my aunt. When I got upset, they would listen to me. I got a lot of my needs met from family and therefore wasn't so dependent upon my husband for everything." Maybe what she was saying is: it takes a village to have a relationship.

Being flexible means having the willingness and ability to change the way you relate to one another as the need arises. The earliest research on healthy family functioning indicates that flexibility—being able to roll with the punches—is a strong predictor of happiness and stability. If you stay with someone past the infatuation stage, your needs—and your partner's needs—will change. And change. And change. Being able to change your expectations and honor your partner's changing needs will enable you to define and redefine love.

Being equitable means being fair about your expectations in a relationship. This may mean sometimes taking turns, going the second mile, or delaying your own gratification to please your partner. Couples who take pleasure in giving as well as receiving have a deeper love and more satisfaction. In terms of defining love through chemistry, compatibility, and commitment, many people will say, "I want it all. I want a relationship with lots of sexual spark, my partner to be my very best friend, and for us to live happily ever after in long-term committed bliss." For this to be possible, you are talking about making the relationship a clear priority in terms of time, energy, and effort. The relationship needs to take precedence over job, career, children, and other outside activities. There are couples who do this but more tend to choose priorities and accept that there are times when sex won't be ecstatic, exclusive moments few and far between, and attention will be going other places in addition to the relationship. However, if you will keep in mind what says "I love you" to your partner and make sure he/she gets this most of the time, you will take the first major step toward building trust, which is the subject of our next chapter.

6

Discovery: Building Trust

TRUE LOVE IS BUILT ON A FOUNDATION OF TRUST

If you asked successful couples, "What holds you together during the times when you are apart either because of distance, busyness, or other commitments?" chances are the word trust would come up. Satisfied couples keep the faith, even in the absence of immediate evidence. This confidence grows out of trust they have built between them. New couples eager to commit sometimes rush past the step of building trust and fail to create a strong connection that will withstand the highs and lows of love. Even partners who have been together for years find they cannot deepen their love, or experience the true joy of a dedicated relationship, without a firm foundation of trust. When you peel away the layers of dissatisfaction in marriage, lack of trust is often at the core. Let's take a closer look at this vital issue and ways to strengthen the integrity of your love.

Right before I began to write this chapter, I was in Chicago making a video for couples that teaches skills for improving relationships. During one of the breaks between taping sessions, I couldn't resist taking advantage of the group's insights, so I posed this question to them: "How would you define trust?"

The first answer came from a handsome, macho guy who spoke up quickly and to the point: "Trust is letting your wife go out with her friends to a bar, and knowing she's not going out to get laid." Though his response was met with laughter, the fact is, many of us do associate trust first and foremost with fidelity, or being sexually faithful, and this certainly is an important way we build trust.

Another woman added a second dimension with her explanation: "Trust is having complete confidence in your partner." Confidence in a relationship grows with consistency over time, so it would seem that being reliable and dependable also helps build trust. A third voice added: "Trust is being able to depend on a person to understand and support you no matter what." In this summation lies the expectation that trust includes being consistent in the specific ways that we need, or where it counts.

They had such energy for the subject that I pushed a little further by asking, "How do you build trust?" The answers came back in various forms:

"Honesty over time."

"Being there to share the bad times as well as the good."

"Getting to really know your partner."

"Being honest about the not so nice stuff. If they'll take that risk, then they will likely be trustworthy."

"Telling your partner what you need and getting it."

So it seems that we build trust by telling the truth, being faithful, sharing the bad times as well as the good, and meeting one another's needs—at least more often than not.

This small group of a half a dozen couples did a fine job of covering the major elements of trust. Their answers came quickly and without disagreement. I find this interesting given the fact that before I began this chapter, I reviewed the relationship books on my shelves and found very little written about trust. Not one—text or trade—had a chapter on building trust, and most didn't have it listed as a topic at all. Yet in my twenty-plus years of working almost exclusively with couples, I find this to be a critical issue. Without trust in the relationship, you live with anxiety, which can lead to conflict, distance, stress, compulsivity, and any number of relational ills.

Examining your level of trust and making necessary corrections is a vital step toward creating true love. Let's look more closely at the elements of trust.

THE TRUTH ABOUT HONESTY

I am often asked, "Is honesty always the best policy?" Knowing that each couple must decide for themselves the level of candor they will practice, I don't attempt to give global advice on this subject; however, I do have a strong opinion about delineating honesty from truth. Honesty has to do with speaking openly and frankly; truth reflects all the facts. Confusing these two causes problems in relationships and can destroy trust. Here is an example.

Grace prided herself on being "a totally honest person." She would return the change to a cashier who gave her too much money, she once drove thirty-eight miles to return the key to a hotel room, and she would be the first person to tell a girlfriend she had gained a few pounds. Unfortunately, Grace was not good at distinguishing honesty from truth, and it caused a great deal of conflict in the beginning of her marriage. On their first visit to the home of Trevor's parents shortly after their wedding, Grace felt uneasy being around his sister and mother. At first it seemed like they were ignoring her and were paying more attention to cooking and running after the children. Then, when she did get their attention, it seemed like they were bossing her and not being friendly. As the family was sitting around the table finishing dinner, Grace decided she would be completely honest with everyone. She chose her words carefully, doing her best not to cast blame. "I know I am new to this family, and I don't want to get off on the wrong foot, but I'm just feeling very uncomfortable here." Everyone stopped eating for a moment and looked at her, then at Trevor, whose face had gone white.

"I'm feeling like there is a lot of tension in this family and nobody is talking about it. I'd rather get it out in the open than to pretend it isn't happening."

Lily, Trevor's sister, was irritated by Grace's comments and responded, "Well, I wasn't feeling any tension, but I am now."

Not to be silenced, Grace pressed on, "I have felt it all day, and I just wanted to say that."

Trevor's father jumped in to change the conversation, "Well, why don't we have dessert and see if that makes us all feel better." With this comment, Trevor spoke, "I'll get the pie. Grace, why don't you come help me."

Once in the kitchen, he said to her, "Please, honey, just let it go. Everyone is nervous about our first visit."

"Well then, why didn't you speak up about your nervousness? You're being just as dishonest as everyone else."

At that moment, Trevor's dad came in and gave Grace a big hug. "I just want you to know we're all glad you came to visit. Now, come on in and enjoy dessert with everyone." He picked up the coffeepot and headed off with Grace and Trevor following.

When Grace spoke at the dinner table, she was being honest about her thoughts and feelings, but her words did not represent the truth. There were some very important facts she overlooked. First, she did not know what other people were feeling; she could only speak for herself. Perhaps more relevant to the situation was another fact: she did not consider the rules of courtesy, nor have compassion for the effect her words would have on the group as a whole.

A larger truth was also ignored: she really wanted to be accepted as a member of Trevor's family and desired to be liked. Her words were not congruent with the whole truth. Her "honesty" did not even represent her own aspirations.

In order to build trust, honesty needs to be consistent with truth. Just because a thought enters your head, or a feeling comes over you, it doesn't mean you have latched on to the truth. You may need to check it out, or gather more information. Words hurt. Impulsive honesty can destroy trust if it is consistently off the mark and stated as fact.

It's been my experience that many individuals are not fully aware of the power of their words on others in their lives. In many cases, the very person who believes he or she has little impact on the partner has sometimes overwhelmed the other person with criticism, judgment, or harshness. The wounded partner's silence—mistaken for ignoring or withdrawal—is often a symptom of overload, fear, and/or hurt.

To build trust, we must be aware that our words are powerful and we can hurt relationships and the people we love. The best way to build trust is to make sure honesty is connected to the truth. To build trust, make sure your words are congruent with your actions and your ultimate goals.

BUILDING TRUST THROUGH FIDELITY

If nothing else, the Bill Clinton–Monica Lewinsky saga gave us food for thought on the subject of fidelity. Over coffee and cocktails, conversations across the country included questions like, "Is it infidelity if you don't have intercourse?" We all got to try our hand at splitting hairs and playing semantics; however, I think there is a much simpler way to determine if you are being unfaithful: simply ask your partner. Can't you hear the president saying, "Hillary, hon, let me run this by you. Would it be okay if . . . ?" I think that simple question could have changed the course of history.

We, too, can keep our history straight by bearing in mind what we have committed to our partner. If you want to know if your behavior is in line with the agreement between the two of you, just ask. Or if asking your spouse doesn't appeal to you, maybe using the definition I learned from a colleague of mine might help. Dr. Shirley Glass defines infidelity as "any activity with a person other than your partner that includes sexual chemistry, emotional intimacy, and elements of secrecy or deception." This means if you are meeting privately with, talking to, or even e-mailing a person you find attractive and keeping the nature of the contact from your partner, then you are being unfaithful and are not building trust.

Why would such a narrow definition be used to delineate fidelity? By keeping our sexual and romantic attention monogamous, we make all our physical and emotional energy available to the relationship. Although you can certainly love more than one person at a time, you cannot be infatuated with more than one person. If romantic interest wanders, the relationship will feel the effects. It can be evidenced in the absence of little nuances between you—the touch of a hand, a thoughtful gesture, romantic excitement, energy, playfulness. Or, because there has been a betrayal, the unfaithful partner will feel some sense of guilt and may, in an attempt to assuage the guilt, look for faults in the partner to justify the infidelity.

The best way to prevent infidelity is to keep your energy focused on your partner and avoid playing around with sexual chemistry. Monogamy is a choice, not an inclination. Each of us can be attracted to more than one person. If you meet enough warm bodies, you will find one that appeals to you, even if you are happy with your present partner. What you do about that is not destiny; it is a personal choice.

FOR BETTER OR FOR WORSE

This adage brings to mind some of life's toughest trials: illness, death, injury, financial hardship, unemployment, family conflict, alcoholism. But according to research, these are not the difficulties that dissolve marriages. It appears that couples are much better prepared for these afflictions than the normal highs and lows of marriage. When there is an immediate danger or a mutual problem to address, couples tend to pull together in a "you and me against the world" fashion. Getting through these trials can bring two people closer and put the importance of the relationship into perspective. However, to build a strong foundation of trust, this same teamwork needs to be applied to the greater threats to marriage: boredom, hopelessness, busyness, and growing apart. When these more silent enemies threaten, the team spirit is needed most.

Tough issues can bring two people closer together—or tear them apart—depending upon how they are handled. If a couple's coping mechanisms include giving up, blaming, shutting down, criticizing, scapegoating, or being compulsively self-sufficient, then chances are difficulties will not build trust.

If obstacles are used to bring out commitment and the two individuals turn to one another for input and suggestion, then problems can become opportunities to draw on your strength as a unit and deepen your trust. Couples who have been together a long time will tell you they each had to do their part to stay connected during the long dry spells. Knowing they can do it again strengthens their trust.

WHEN IT'S TOUGH TO TRUST

Most people start out a relationship with a basic sense of trust. They see the other as honest, faithful, and dependable and take the stance "innocent until proven guilty." But there are individuals who, because of earlier experiences, have difficulty trusting. They begin a relationship with a basic sense of mistrust, although it may not always be conscious. It's important to recognize your own ability—or inability—to trust others in order to make sure you can separate your history from current events; otherwise, you might judge someone in your present for a crime committed against you by someone else in the past.

Use the following exercise to look closely at your history regarding the issues of trust.

EARLY TRUST

Answer true (T) or false (F) to the following statements:

_____ 1. I believe most people can be trusted.

_____ 2. I find it easy to trust those close to me.

_____ 3. The people I have loved the most have been trustworthy.

_____ 4. The people closest to me throughout my life have been sensitive to my needs.

_____ 5. I was raised with very responsible people.

_____ 6. I have several models of happy love relationships in my family.

_____ 7. Growing up, I could trust the adults in my family to tell the truth.

_____ 8. Communication was very clear in our family.

_____ 9. As a child, I was given good information about life.

_____10. Telling the truth was an important value in our family.

_____11. I could always trust my mother to care for me.

_____12. I could always trust my father to care for me.

_____13. I felt important growing up.

_____14. My earliest romantic relationships were fulfilling.

_____15. I felt attractive growing up.

_____16. I got very good sex education as a child and adolescent.

_____17. I came into adulthood very well prepared for relationships.

_____18. I felt special as a child.

_____19. My parents were devoted to one another.

_____20. I have always been trustworthy.

Total number of true (T) answers: _____

Having completed the early trust checklist, what are your thoughts?

TRUST HISTORY

Circle the answer that completes the sentence most accurately. Circle more than one if they fit. If none applies, complete the sentence on your own.

1. **My biggest difficulty with trust has been:**

    a. not trusting enough

    b. trusting people who are not trustworthy

    c. expecting people to be perfect

    d. not trusting myself

2. **In terms of jealousy, I:**

    a. am rarely jealous

    b. am prone to jealousy

    c. have a jealous partner

    d. like it when my partner is jealous

3. **My personal history with trust includes:**

    a. being untrustworthy

    b. breaking confidences

    c. being very trustworthy

    d. learning to be more trustworthy

4. **I am least trustworthy with:**

    a. private information

    b. money

    c. keeping appointments

    d. sexual fidelity

5. My greatest fears around trust have to do with:

a. sex

b. money

c. friends

d. family

6. Most of my love relationships have been:

a. trustworthy

b. fulfilling

c. disappointing

d. painful

7. In a relationship, I am usually the one who:

a. wins the arguments

b. gets his/her way

c. apologizes

d. gives in

8. My worst fear in a relationship is:

a. getting hurt

b. hurting the other person

c. getting too close

d. losing interest

9. In a relationship, I practice:

a. total honesty and truth

b. selective honesty

c. the right to privacy

d. prying into my partner's privacy

10. **Overall, my ability to trust is:**

   a. healthy and balanced
   b. comfortable for me
   c. still developing
   d. insecure

TRUST AFFECTS SATISFACTION

There are no right or wrong answers in the two previous exercises. They are designed to help you look at your past, as well as your present, issues with trust. Going back over your answers, how would you evaluate your history with trust? Can you see any reflection of your history in your current relationship(s)?

If you have had difficulty trusting important people in your life, it could easily be affecting your satisfaction today. Individuals who have been let down before sometimes mistrust even a trustworthy person, or overreact to issues of trust. If you suspect this may be the case with you, check it out with two or three dependable people. Ask them for feedback. You might also consult your partner about how trust issues show up in your relationship. Or, ask yourself these questions:

1. Am I a perfectionist in my expectations of others?
2. Do I overreact when my partner disappoints me in the least?
3. Am I considered controlling by people who know me well?
4. Am I frequently looking for ways that my partner disappoints me?
5. Do I focus on the negative aspects of our relationship far more than the positives?
6. Am I difficult to please?
7. Am I hard on myself?

8. Am I judgmental of those close to me?
9. Do I tend to trust the wrong people?
10. Do I find it hard to accept that I am wrong?

If you answered yes to three or more of these questions, this chapter will be important for you.

BUILDING TRUST THROUGH CONSISTENCY AND DEPENDABILITY

Even if you have had difficulty with trust in the past, you can learn it at any time in your life. The best way to do this is through being consistently dependable yourself, and spending time with others who do the same.

There are three steps to this process:

Step 1: Say what you are going to do.

Step 2: Do it.

Step 3: Repeat steps 1 and 2.

Being true to your word is the key to building trust. I've seen many couples struggle with this issue of dependability. Many commitments go astray shortly after step 1. Words never make it into action. Out of the desire to please—or fear of saying no—one partner will make a promise, but not keep it. The promise may have been in response to a request that was unreasonable to begin with, but instead of saying, "That's not possible," a commitment is made, only to be broken. Words followed by inaction spell mistrust. If you can't rely on your partner, it's difficult to believe he/she cares. No matter how much love is professed, unless it shows up in consistent behavior, you don't feel loved.

It's far better to say no and be trustworthy than to say yes and be unreliable. It is also better to make a small commitment you know you can keep rather than a bigger one you'll likely break. The process of making a promise and following through is more important than the magnitude of the act.

SCRATCH WHERE IT ITCHES!

We have one of those family stories passed down through the generations about my Uncle Jerry, who, as a young boy, ran to his mama complaining about his back itching. As she did her best to respond to his frantic directions of "Higher, lower," she just couldn't give him relief. Finally, in desperation he said, "Mama, just scratch where it itches!"

Isn't this what we would love to have—someone who can scratch where it itches, who knows us well enough to consistently meet our needs at just the right time, and without much instruction? Dependability counts the most when it hits the mark. You get bonus points for accuracy. The way to increase the likelihood you will get your needs met is to be clear about the trust issues related to the important areas in your life.

Complete the following sentences to explore the issues of trust.

Information for your partner:

1. I would feel more secure in our relationship if . . .

2. I would trust you more if . . .

3. I would be willing to risk more in terms of romance if . . .

4. I would take more sexual risks with you if . . .

5. I would trust you more sexually if . . .

6. I would feel better about us going out together socially if . . .

7. I would feel closer to you emotionally if . . .

8. I would do more projects with you if . . .

9. I would enjoy time with our family more if . . .

10. The one thing that would strengthen my commitment the most is . . .

Now, explore how you can be more trustworthy to your partner:

1. I believe you would trust me more if I . . .

2. Romantically, I could increase the trust between us if I . . .

3. Sexually, I could increase the trust if I . . .

4. I could improve the trust level of our friendship if I . . .

5. I could make our relationship safer if I . . .

6. I could make our social life more fun if I . . .

7. I could make it easier to live with me if I . . .

8. I could improve our time with family if I . . .

9. I could make our relationship emotionally safer for you if I . . .

10. I could make projects around home more enjoyable if I . . .

Defining love, as explained in Chapter 5, is designed to help you be specific about what you and your partner expect from your relationship. In order to build trust, you must be consistent in the ways it counts the most. Look at the following checklist to evaluate your trustworthiness in meeting the specific needs of your partner.

CAN I BE TRUSTED?

Looking at the areas of chemistry, compatibility, and commitment, rate your trustworthiness in meeting your partner's needs and expectations. Answer yes (Y) or no (N), doing your best to include your partner's point of view.

Chemistry:

_____ 1. I am sexually faithful.

_____ 2. My partner would approve of how I act without him/ her.

_____ 3. I encourage my partner to take sexual risks with me.

_____ 4. My partner can count on me to keep our relationship romantic.

_____ 5. I am honest with my partner about my sexual needs.

_____ 6. I am kind and sensitive when addressing the sexual issues in our relationship.

_____ 7. I make an effort to keep myself attractive.

_____ 8. I keep the details of our sex life totally confidential.

_____ 9. I am realistic about my sexual expectations.

_____10. I am a patient lover.

Total yes (Y) answers: _____

Compatibility:

_____ 1. I do a good job of keeping my partner up to date with information.

_____ 2. My partner would say that I am an understanding friend.

_____ 3. I tell my partner things no one else knows.

_____ 4. I do my best to make sure my partner and I have fun together.

_____ 5. I include my partner in the important events in my life.

_____ 6. I make it a point to be a good sport about activities that my partner enjoys that I don't.

_____ 7. I am very reliable about doing my part at home.

_____ 8. I do my part to help resolve conflict.

_____ 9. Our home is a better place to live because of my efforts.

_____10. My partner would say that I rarely criticize.

Total yes (Y) answers: _____

Commitment:

_____ 1. I am 100 percent committed to my relationship.

_____ 2. I'm the one who usually gets us back on track when our relationship hits a low spot.

_____ 3. My partner feels confident about my commitment to us.

_____ 4. I show appreciation for my partner's commitment to us.

_____ 5. I take a positive, active part in family activities.

_____ 6. Our relationship is an inspiration to others.

_____ 7. I am very aware when our relationship needs attention.

_____ 8. I make our relationship a priority.

_____ 9. My partner would say that I make our relationship a priority.

_____10. I am happy with the roles we play in our relationship.

Total yes (Y) answers: _____

Total score _____ **out of a possible 60**

TRUST IS THE FOUNDATION

Trust comes with consistency over time, and you'll get the most love mileage out of being trustworthy in the areas important to your partner. If you adhere to the truth, use honesty with caution, are faithful, consistent, and reliable, and you hang in there during the tough times, you'll build trust and a strong foundation for true love. Building trust is the last lesson in discovery. Once you've learned these essential, relationship-building skills, you're ready to deepen your commitment and your connection to your partner in the most advanced stage of lasting love.

7

The Connection Stage:
Expanding Commitment

Commitment gives you the opportunity to be truly known by another human being. Today marriage and commitment are getting a lot of bad press. We are constantly reminded about the high divorce rate and the fact that marriage is at an all time low. Increasing numbers of young people—having lived through the divorce of their parents, family, or friends—are speaking out about their shattered illusions concerning marriage and are avoiding commitment altogether. Sadly, many will never know the joy and satisfaction that can come from dedicating oneself to long-term love. Pundits and politicians offer a lot of "shoulds" and "oughts" about marriage, but what we don't hear enough about is the sheer joy and delight of committed love. When a celebrity gets a divorce it makes the front page, but I've yet to see an anniversary make the headlines. It's not that these happy marriages don't exist. Tony D. Burton wrote a little book called *These Are a Few of My Favorite Things* to benefit the Make-A-Wish Foundation. The content of the book is simply a compilation of handwritten responses from famous—as well as not-so-famous—people answering the question, "What are your favorite things?" I was struck by how many well-known people referred to time with their partner in their answers.

Here are some excerpts:

Carl Reiner—"helping my wife cook dinner"

Florence Henderson—"the love and respect of my husband"

Jeff Gordon—"spending a nice quiet evening with my wife, Brooke"

Bob Dole—"Sunday brunch with Elizabeth"

Maria Shriver—"cuddling with my husband"

James Carville—"hanging out with my wife"

Tracy Austin—"a quiet dinner with my husband"

Ann Curry—"holding my husband's hand"

Robin Williams—"feeling the warmth that my wife's laughter brings"

Fortunately, you don't have to be rich and famous to experience the deep love that commitment brings. Take these examples of everyday people showing their loyalty:

- Bonnie wrote her husband every day for a year while he was stationed in the Persian Gulf.

- Cindie supported Mike while he struggled with his start-up company.

- Gene worked a second job so his wife, Vickie, could quit work and get her RN certification.

- Jasmyn and Julian take turns getting up with the baby at night.

- Chris arranged for all six of Brandon's brothers and sisters to surprise him with a visit on his fortieth birthday.

- Bill worked thirty-three years of shift work in an aluminum plant so that his wife, Martha, could live near and take care of her parents.

- Jewel wakes up every morning and asks herself, "How can I show love to my husband today?"

- Brian says a prayer of thanks every night for his wife and family.

- Tony and Maggie, after fifty-three years together, still go to sleep in the spoon position.

- Alice sings to her husband at night when he's had a stressful day and can't sleep.

- Terry, in the midst of running a start-up business, finds time to call her partner every day just to say "I love you."

There are millions and millions of love stories that go on every day without acclaim.

A CLOSER LOOK AT COMMITMENT

Many people think of commitment as one-dimensional: you're committed to each other or you're not. In this context, commitment simply refers to staying together. If you have already made the decision to stay with your current partner and share this point of view, you might look upon this chapter as unnecessary. However, commitment involves much more than showing up at the same residence and representing yourselves as a couple. There are two categories of commitment: commitment to being together and commitment to the relationship. In order to expand your commitment and deepen your connection, it's necessary to look at both dimensions.

Scott Stanley, Ph.D., and his colleagues from the University of Denver have given us the finest research pertaining to the heart of commitment. Their findings reveal a clear distinction between what they call "constraint commitment" and "dedicated commitment." Constraint commitment refers to staying in a relationship because you don't want to deal with the consequences of getting out, such as losing money, splitting property, relinquishing status, disappointing others, and/or being single. On the other hand, dedicated commitment involves staying together because of gratification resulting from your investment in the relationship. Individuals who are dedicated do their part to ensure that the relationship is satisfying for both people. They protect it from outside forces by the way they think, act, and prioritize their life. Dedicated commitment is a part of true love; constraint commitment is not.

COMMITMENT WITHOUT MARRIAGE

More than 50 percent of couples who marry live together first, and with far more societal acceptance than in years past. Researchers Lynne Casper and Liana Sayer have found that cohabitation has different meaning to different couples—and the meaning they give the arrangement predicts whether the relationship will endure or go by the wayside. Couples who use cohabiting as a substitute for marriage tend not to marry and experience separation at a greater rate than married couples. Those who are certain about their partner as well as marriage do tend to wed, whereas those that are uncertain about a partner but certain about marriage tend to split up—usually within eighteen months. The major difference between commitment in a marriage and in a cohabiting relationship is that marriage forms a new unit. Cohabiting is more like being roommates with sex; the attitudes are more individualistic and less relationship-oriented. Generally speaking, the commitment is not as great or enduring in cohabitation as it is in marriage. Of course there are many exceptions to this rule. The bottom line is the dedication of both partners.

If you are simply putting in time with your relationship or staying because of constraints, this will not lead to deep connection. You may stay together, especially if your partner shares the constraints, but don't expect to be happy. If you are living with a wandering eye and are constantly searching for your partner's shortcomings, true love will elude you. The only way you can have any hope of changing your relationship is by changing yourself. Here's how you can begin.

DO SOME SERIOUS SOUL SEARCHING

If you've ever been unhappy in your job situation, you know how it affects your performance and commitment. Or, if you have a co-worker who isn't committed to the job, it can taint the entire work environment. It can make your workload heavier and affect your job satisfaction. Commitment, and a lack of it, has a subtle way of affecting every aspect of relationships, whether at work or at home. It shows up in the little things, like being late, giving only the minimum amount of effort, forgetting, procrastinating, and generally having a bad attitude.

How is your attitude about your relationship? Do you sit around focusing on your partner's faults and shortcomings? Are you waiting for him/her to change? Are you second-guessing your commitment? Do you dream about former partners? Do you have fantasies of exit or even a getaway plan? Are you open to the romantic interests of other people? Do you have one foot out the door? When commitment is in question there is no safety in a relationship. This means that each person in the relationship lives in a state of heightened alert and is likely to overreact to the smallest of issues.

COMMITMENT TO THE RELATIONSHIP

Sean felt sure that he would never love another woman like he loved Emily. They had met on a rock-climbing expedition, and her athletic ability, obvious intelligence, and rugged beauty immediately struck him. At first he was intimidated by her skill and well-rounded competence, but after a few conversations her effusive sense of humor and ability to laugh at herself put him at ease. As they got acquainted, he was delighted to find that they both were from the same general area in D.C. and lived only two train stops apart. After their weekend meeting and three more dates, Sean realized that he could easily fall for this woman—and he eventually did. However, that is not the end of the story.

Emily, the mother of twin daughters, had divorced their father three years ago when he announced that he was in love with another woman. For the good of the children, Emily agreed not only to share custody with her ex, but that they would stay in the same geographic location until the children were out of high school, which was eight years away. Emily's father had been a career military man and she knew how difficult it was to move several times throughout your formative years.

Sean, on the other hand, was slated for a managerial position in a local supermarket chain and the only way he could move up was to relocate. He was also unsure as to whether he wanted children. Each time he and Emily were out with the girls, he found himself being impatient and even jealous of her divided attention. More and more he wanted just to spend time with her alone, but every other weekend the girls were present. After many long conversations, Sean realized that despite how much he loved Emily, he was not ready to choose the lifestyle that went with her. For a period of time they tried just being friends, but his attraction to her was too strong. He found that the only way he could move on with his life was to move on without Emily.

WHEN YOU CHOOSE A PARTNER, YOU CHOOSE A LIFESTYLE

Deciding to commit to a marriage or permanent relationship may be the most important decision of your life. This choice will likely influence where you live, how much money you have, the friends and family you relate to, whether you have children, how you are seen in the wider community, and your overall happiness. A satisfying relationship is the single greatest predictor of success in life. On the contrary, an unhappy relationship can make your life miserable and taint most other aspects of your life. In fact, dissatisfied relationships result in a multibillion-dollar cost to taxpayers each year in time lost at work, low productivity, illness, violence, and crime—not to mention the acting out behaviors of the affected children.

Shae Zeldin was dreading the holidays. Each year she fantasized about going to some desert island where no one could find her until they were all over. Although she enjoyed parts of them, she did not like the inevitable arguments that would occur between her and her husband, Lester, over anything from what kind of stuffing to put into the Thanksgiving turkey, to who would end up buying and wrapping the presents for Hanukkah. To make matters worse, they had fallen into the habit of using the company of others to take below-the-belt punches at one another. Last year it got so bad that their oldest son, Miles, went to spend the night with friends even though his favorite cousin was visiting. He was gone for twelve hours without letting them know his whereabouts. Benjie, their other child, would just withdraw into his room when the bickering started.

It's not that Shae and Lester were unaware of their bad habits, nor did either of them like them. They were just caught in a trap where each had a hair-trigger and the other knew how to pull it. Each time they vowed not to go there, they did it again. Even though Shae fantasized about leaving Lester, she knew she never would. Divorce was not an option in her family, but in tough times she did think of herself being a young widow.

This may sound like an exaggerated example, but many of you know this is very real. When Thoreau wrote "the mass of men lead lives of quiet desperation," he could have been describing the existence of many couples. Can you imagine for a moment how Shae's ambivalence toward her marriage affects her life, her health, and her attitude toward others—not to mention her attitude toward her husband and the marriage? Yet most people would look at the Zeldins as a committed couple—and they would be technically correct. Shae and Lester both would say they intend to stay together. You and I know many couples who, despite the quality of their relationship, stay together until the bitter end (pun intended). True love involves far more than this. Your soul has to be dedicated to the relationship, as well as your body.

QUESTIONS TO PONDER ABOUT YOUR COMMITMENT

Now take a closer, more soul-searching look at your commitment by pondering the questions that follow. I suggest you answer them without writing, because I want you to really think about your answers and be as honest as possible. Dig down deep into your psyche. Do your best to be thorough in your responses. By doing so you will get a clear picture of your current commitment, which can give direction for expanding your love.

Are you certain that this is the person you want to spend the rest of your life with?

If somehow you inherited fifty million dollars, would you stay in this relationship?

If you knew that you could be in a relationship with any other person who would love you undyingly, is this the partner you would still choose?

If you knew for sure you were going to live to age one hundred and be in good health, is this the person you would want to spend the rest of your life with?

Are you a person who generally keeps commitments?

When you look at other couples, do you compare your relationship favorably?

Have the two of you combined your money?

Are you completely honest about your spending?

Do you consult each other on important matters?

Have you closed your mind to pursuing attraction to others?

Do you see yourself with this person throughout life?

Do you believe this person is the love of your life?

Do you automatically think as a couple?

Do you weigh personal decisions against implications for you and your partner?

Do you and your partner consult with one another on a regular basis?

Do you compare your partner favorably with all others?

Are large possessions viewed as jointly owned?

Do your friends support your relationship?

Does your family support your relationship?

Do you speak favorably about your relationship to your closest friends?

Are you married?

Have you had a ceremony acknowledging your commitment?

Do you represent yourself to other people as committed?

Do you wear a wedding ring?

Do you have a joint will?

In the case of death, have you made arrangements together?

Do you think of this person as your soul mate or the best match you could find?

If you had a chance to start over, would you start with this person?

Do you and your partner treat your relationship as a priority?

Do the two of you make joint decisions on major matters?

Do you keep each other informed?

Are you dependable to your partner?

Do your fantasies include your partner?

Do you believe that you and your partner are an outstanding match?

Do you put concerted effort into improving your relationship?

Are you willing to postpone some of your personal dreams for the good of the relationship?

Do you take responsibility for repairing damage to your relationship?

Do you monitor your behavior for the good of the relationship?

Do you take your partner seriously?

Do you listen to your partner?

Do you and your partner discuss the future often?

Does your behavior clearly show that your relationship is a priority?

Do you give as well as receive help in your relationship?

Do you focus on pleasing your partner more than being pleased?

Do you focus more on the positive aspects of your relationship than the negatives?

Would it be really difficult for you to lose this relationship?

Are you against divorce/separation?

Do you feel 100 percent clear about staying in this relationship?

The point of answering these provocative questions is to make you aware of any reluctance you might have about your present commitment. Do I think you have to answer yes to all the questions to be committed? No, of course not. Every relationship is different. However, it's been my experience that commitment is a bottom-line issue. If you are unsure whether you are in or out of the relationship, then love cannot deepen and happiness will elude you. It is very important to be honest with yourself about your level of dedication.

Logan and Carmen had been married for six years, and most of that time had been rocky. This was the second marriage for both and neither wanted another divorce. But try as they might, they could not get the relationship stabilized. They came to me after a big fight that had ended with threats of leaving.

Logan was a very bright, articulate man who was easily provoked by Carmen's intense expression of feelings. She was equally exasperated by his cool exterior, which she took for lack of interest. It didn't take long during the first session for their core issue to surface. Carmen fired the first rocket by accusing Logan of never being committed to the relationship. When he heard this, he just shook his head and said, "Carmen, I don't know what to say to that. Words have never helped . . ." They both went silent. She started to cry; he stared out the window.

"Have you been through this before?" I asked. They nodded in affirmation. I continued, "Then let me ask you both a question. If one of you were to leave, who would it be?" Logan looked at Carmen expectantly. She looked back at him, first with a blank stare, then with a sense of awareness.

"It would be me," said Carmen, obviously surprised by her own answer. "I would leave, not you."

"That's right," Logan affirmed with a gentle smile.

The three of us just sat there and let the reality of the truth sink in. It was not the first time I had heard one partner blame the other for what she didn't know was in her own mind.

Sometimes you blame your partner for an idea that lives in you. After reading and answering the questions on the previous couple of pages, you should have a clearer picture of where you need to begin to expand your commitment.

THE FEAR OF COMMITMENT

Commitment means you have the right to expect your partner to meet some of your needs some of the time. People who avoid commitment often do not want to give that right. They may fear that their partner's needs are too great, or their ability to respond is too small. Sometimes they avoid commitment out of fear of connection. Whatever the reason, fear of commitment will prevent deep connection with your partner. Here are some helpful ways to overcome your fears, deepen your commitment, and live with more satisfaction.

FOCUS ON THE POSITIVE

Every year during the first weekend of December, my friend Suzanne Schmidt and I conduct a personal growth weekend for women. This year Linda Eaves, who always attends and is a member of the group called "The Wild Bunch," told of an exercise from *Simple Abundance Journal of Gratitude* by Sarah Ban Breathnach that changed her life. First thing every morning for a year, she has written in a journal five things she is grateful for. Linda encouraged all of us to try this simple activity, and by the radiant look on her face this year, she made me a believer! Later I realized that I could elaborate on this exercise by making it a point to include gratitude for my partner each morning as I count my other blessings.

GIVE ASSURANCE

Sometimes you can deepen your own commitment, while at the same time help your partner expand his/her commitment, by giving assurance. No matter how long you have been together it is still good to hear "I love you and I intend to spend the rest of my life with you." In my work with couples I often ask the question, "What is your contract with each other, that is, the commitment to your relationship?" Although I often get blank stares at first, I sit and wait for someone to say aloud, "Well, we are committed and intend to stay committed." When these words are verbalized there is often a nonverbal sigh of relief accompanied by an infusion of hope. It makes my job easier and the couple more motivated to improve the quality of their relationship.

FUTURE TALK

Another way couples can expand their commitment is through talking about and making plans for the future. This can include simple plans like taking a day trip, or major plans like building a house. Or, you can deepen your commitment by setting common goals for the relationship. Have you taken stock of your goals lately? Do you two have a mutual vision? What do you hope to accomplish together within the next year? What about the next five years? Discussing the future sends the message that you intend to stay together.

A few days ago when I was getting my nails done, a woman named Carol was sitting at the station next to me and Karen, my manicurist, mentioned that she and her husband were getting ready to leave for Austria. Having been there myself years ago I turned to her and asked, "What made you choose Austria—other than the obvious reasons?"

"Well, that's a good story," she replied. "It came about from a promise my husband, Ron, made to me forty years ago. We were out on a date, eating dinner in a restaurant, and "The Blue Danube" was playing. He looked at me and said, 'Someday I'll take you there.' This past March was the fortieth anniversary of that date. To be honest with you, I had forgotten about it, but he hadn't. In commemoration of that promise he presented me with tickets to Austria and told me he's doing this so I would know he is a man of his word."

This couple's future talk ultimately became a dream come true.

COMMEMORATE YOUR ANNIVERSARY

I once met a couple on an airplane who were flying to Hawaii to get married for the eleventh time! Every year they "married" each other again, only in a different location. They repeated their vows, had a ceremony, and truly celebrated every year. They had been married underwater, in an airplane, in Las Vegas, on a cruise ship, on Bourbon Street, on top of a ski slope—you get the picture. They had the best time telling me about their ritual and I enjoyed hearing about it.

"Commemorate" means to keep alive; that's the purpose of the anniversary. When you think about it, your anniversary should be the best holiday of the year. Why not make it that way if it is not? Think what a statement that would make about your relationship.

SHOW YOUR COMMITMENT

Love has no legs. Without deeds, loving someone is not always enough to keep a relationship together. Commitment is made manifest in actions. One of the best ways you can demonstrate commitment is by making your partner's needs a priority in the areas that touch his/her heart the most. This may mean putting your own needs on hold for a while, giving when you'd rather not, or going the extra mile. This could mean:

> Having sex when you're not in the mood.
> Eating a snack when you want real food.
> Watching a love story instead of the game.
> Trying something different when you prefer the same.
> Going to the in-laws when you'd rather stay home.
> Sharing private articles such as hairbrush or comb.
> Talking about the relationship when you prefer to sleep.
> Letting him tell the story without making a peep.
> Leaving work at the office—being home by six.
> Hiking in the woods when you're afraid of ticks.
> Making the coffee when you don't even drink it.
> Walking miles in the mall for some little trinket.
> Keeping silent when you want to give direction.
> Getting up in the night to show your protection.
> Sleeping close when you prefer space.
> Living with plaid when you prefer lace.
> And making it clear that your love is true
> By sharing each day "I love you."

Commitment takes on many forms but in order to assure your partner of your commitment, you need to make your intentions clear. You can do this by showing love in the ways that touch your partner most. You can acknowledge the ways your partner shows his/her dedication and expresses appreciation. You can clarify your own intentions and make sure they are reflected in your actions and attitude. And finally, you can focus on the positives in your relationship by showing gratitude as you look forward to a future together.

DEDICATED COMMITMENT OVER TIME
LEADS TO TRUE LOVE

In an interview with *Glamour* magazine I used the term true love, and the writer asked what I meant by that. In part of my answer I said, "True love has stood the test of time. It has weathered many storms and come through some rough times. It has proven itself strong enough to withstand periods of neglect due to other commitments. It is a love that can find sexual attraction not only in a young supple body, but in one that is wrinkled and showing age spots. True love has ripened with commitment and shows up in the privacy of everyday life in the little acts of kindness and intimate gestures."

Much of the knowledge I gained about true love emerged when I interviewed over 1,500 couples for my book *Hot Monogamy*. I found that the most satisfied and deeply committed people are ordinary, like those you see at the mall or the grocery store. It's as if they have a delicious secret. In fact, I discovered that one of the reasons we don't hear many of their love stories is that this type of commitment and deep connection is very private and precious. The committed love of another human being is one of the unique experiences of life and often difficult to describe in words. The remainder of this book will focus on deepening connection and provide direction for making it a sacred part of your life.

8

Connection: Deepening Connection

Even though Connection is the last stage of love, the course of true love does not end here. Intimate connection energizes you, and takes you to heights beyond even the high of infatuation. Then, inspired by the energy between you, your relationship begins again—first revisiting the glory of fresh love, then on to discovery and back to an even deeper connection. Once you have established the connection of true love, you no longer get caught in the doldrums of post-rapture. Of course you still face disappointments and disagreements, but it is with the confidence that your love will see you through. Each time you move through the highs and lows of love you return to a deeper level of love. The truth about love is that it just gets better and better with time.

During the Infatuation Stage, couples experience long periods of connection. They talk, listen, touch, have fun, and take pleasure in life's ordinary occurrences. A simple event like dinner can last for hours extended by lengthy conversation, silent gazing, and sensual exchanges. Under the influence of nature's love cocktail, intimate contact is effortless. Even when apart, lovers stay connected through fantasy, anticipation, or thinking of ways to please one another. These frequent experiences of caring deepen the connection between the two and eventually become part of the phenomenon we call love.

A simple way to understand connection is to think of it as two people sharing an experience. You touch me, I feel your touch. You talk, I listen, and vice versa. Individuals make connection by paying attention and tuning in to one another—as well as what they are doing. It's as if for a moment there are no barriers between you. Each has access to the other's energy, which creates synergy and intensifies the experience. This is why watching a ball game together is more fun than watching it alone, and having sex is more pleasurable when both of you are interested.

THE ORIGIN OF CONNECTION

Life begins with connection when the egg and the sperm combine to form the human embryo. While in utero, the fetus experiences the perfect state of connection. From the moment of her first breath, baby begins moving toward contact because she innately knows: without connection there is no life. Donald Winnicott, noted infant researcher, once stated, "There's no such thing as a baby." What he meant by that was an infant cannot survive without a caregiver. If babies are not touched, held, caressed, stimulated, and otherwise cared for, they fail to grow.

Because connection is necessary for our survival, it is reinforced by the release of neuropeptides, which create feelings of calm, comfort, and emotional well-being. When we get close to someone we trust, these delightful neurotransmitters make us feel delight. Separation, on the other hand, because it threatened our survival as an infant, sends a message of alarm and triggers adrenaline release, making us anxious and uneasy.

As adults we come to understand that we can survive alone, and we become more comfortable with separation, even enjoy periods of it. Despite this fact, throughout our lives we still long for contact and want to be near someone who cares for us. It may not always look that way, but all humans long to be connected to other humans. The longing to be connected is a drive deep within us. It is not an option. While infants need connection to survive, adults need connection to thrive.

ADULT CONNECTION

The most significant connection in adulthood is between partners. Friends, children, even parents cannot meet our needs the
way a spouse can. The roles partners play with each other cover a
wider range. They can be lovers, best friends, confidants, social
partners, financial partners, housemates, and teammates. The
primary love relationship is sensual, sexual, social, domestic, supportive, exclusive, and committed. People have said to me,
"Well, my friends are more committed to me than my partner." I
say to that, "Start requiring of your friends what you require of a
partner. Try saying, 'I want you here at the house every night at six
o'clock, and I expect you to contribute to half the housework and
half the income. In addition, you have to put up with me at my
worst.' Then see how committed your friends are." Friendships
are important to a rich, full life, but the primary love relationship
goes far beyond friendship. The comprehensive nature of a committed love relationship gives it conscious and unconscious importance. When you connect with a partner he or she becomes a
primary source of your security. There are several reasons for
this. First of all, the commitment gives you the assurance of having someone who is on your side, in your corner, and who—when
push comes to shove—is there for you. Second, the connecting
activities that go on between two partners—like touching, holding, listening, and supporting—all produce the release of endorphins. These wonderful natural opiates give you a sense of calm
and tranquillity. Through ongoing connection, your life becomes
less stressful; your breathing slows down and your body relaxes.
Because of this calming effect, your relationship becomes a
haven—a respite—from the outside world. You go through life
with more ease and comfort when connected to a loving partner.

HOW CONNECTED ARE YOU?

Since it is clear that we all long for connection, the question is: How connected are you to your partner?

Use the following questions to explore this subject. How often do you . . .

Feel the sense of working as team toward a common goal?

Have a serious disagreement, then make up with little effort?

Look in your partner's eyes and get a rush?

Share a good laugh?

Tell your partner just how much you care?

Feel comforted by your partner's presence when under outside stress?

Get a thrill from your partner's touch?

Miss your partner when you are apart?

Feel your partner's support?

Experience pleasure at the sight of your partner?

Feel moved by your partner's thoughtfulness?

Enjoy the feel of your partner's body?

Get engrossed in a pleasant activity the two of you are sharing?

Experience tears of joy with your partner?

Feel touched by your partner's vulnerability?

Feel connected to your partner from a distance?

Feel calmed by the comfort of your relationship?

Feel comforted lying next to your partner?

Have the experience of being in love with your partner?

Feel appreciation for the fact that your partner is in your life?

If you answered "often" to most of these questions, you probably have a deep connection with your partner. But if you had to think about your answers, or search for the last memory, then it may be that you are like many who still have something important to learn about meaningful contact. You cannot deepen love without connection, and it's never too late to learn how to do this. Let's take a closer look at how this can be done.

FEAR OF CONNECTION

Often during wedding ceremonies, the bride and groom light a unity candle. Taking their individual candles, they light a larger candle that represents their marriage. Before I understood the true meaning of connection, I didn't like this ritual because at the point of lighting the unity candle, the minister would usually say "And the two became one." As a person who fears being controlled, I wondered "Which one?" Now that I know the truth about love, I understand this ritual much better. The ceremony reflects the creation of a third entity—the relationship—not symbiosis, fusion, or one person controlling the other. Neither individual flame is extinguished by lighting the unity candle, and when each is taken away, it shines just as bright as it did before. The unity candle signifies that, with commitment, there are not just two people to consider, but a third—the relationship.

My earlier reaction to the candle ceremony represents a common fear concerning connection: "If I let myself get close to you I will lose my freedom and sacrifice my individuality." However, connection related to true love requires that you maintain your identity. If you give up your identity, that is, your opinions, your desires, your ideas, you will bring little or nothing to the relationship. It takes two people, bringing their individual personalities and talent, to provide enough energy for managing the highs and lows of life, as well as love.

The second most common fear concerning connection is fear of loss: "If I let myself get close to you and then you leave me, that would be devastating." The human condition includes the ability to not only survive loss, but to love again and again. Loneliness is the belief that there is only one source of love. The truth is that love is all around you. You just need the courage to let it in.

These two common fears, of being controlled and being left, keep many people from experiencing true love. However, the most common fear of connection is caused by the fear of getting what you want! When you really want something and long for it—as we all do for connection—it becomes a painful subject. To go without connection is uncomfortable because we are designed to be in a close relationship, it's the nature of our species. The longer you go without connection, the more you begin to associate it with pain. Once you begin to associate connection with pain, the closer you get to someone, the more uncomfortable you feel. So even if you want to get close, when you try, you feel uncomfortable. This discomfort makes you resist the very thing you want. You can probably think of times when you have been your own worst enemy in a relationship. When you spoiled an intimate moment—or got very close to letting yourself be vulnerable, then pulled away. No doubt you have also seen this pattern in your partner.

The fear of getting what you want is part of reunion grief, a complex psychological process that frequently thwarts the course of true love. Reunion grief has several facets. As stated, when you finally get something you've wanted for a long time, your anxiety goes up because your psyche associates it with pain. In order to get past this fear and on to the good feelings, you first have to override your brain telling you "Don't go there, it's painful!" After you get through this first hurdle—accepting what you have longed for—the phenomenon of reunion grief is not over. Once you have the courage to step across the line and let yourself be loved, the longing ends, but the grief begins. When you finally get the love you long for, you begin to grieve for all the years you lived without it. This is why a beautiful experience can move you to tears. Like in any crisis or stressful situation, when you are in the middle of it, you are coping; you don't have time to grieve. But when the crisis is over, that's when the strong feelings come up. The best example of this can be seen with little children. Say, little Johnny has been with grandpa all day. When dad comes to pick him up, within the first few minutes he'll show anger or cry. Grandpa might say, "Why, Johnny, you've been having a great time all day long, what's the matter?" The answer: reunion grief. All day long Johnny has been coping with missing his dad. When dad finally shows up, the longing ends and the grief begins. Johnny's anger and tears are a normal part of reunion grief.

Those of us who have spent many years without intimate connection, either from childhood or since a previous relationship, have a special challenge. Without an understanding of reunion grief, when true love arrives, we may find ourselves second-guessing, feeling numb, shutting down, being irritable, and ultimately disconnecting from someone we love. We need tremendous courage to manage the anxiety built up over all the years of longing. The truth about love is that getting what you want is both pleasurable and challenging. If you do not understand its nature, you can push love away when it comes to call. Most of us are not aware of how we are keeping love and connection at bay, so let's look at some common disconnecting behaviors.

DISCONNECTION

When two people fear connection and lack connecting skills, they find ways to avoid closeness. With two strong-minded people, this can look like an all-out war with each battle ending in serious threats of separation or divorce. But more often, couples use cold war tactics like isolation and withdrawal. They go about living separate lives, staying busy with individual activities. These parallel relationships can go on for years in a state of lonely silence. In the following example, we see that this is where the Gonzaleses' marriage was headed.

Tino and Pilar met at an office party in December. Their first formal date was on New Year's Eve and they saw each other steadily from that point. Their courtship was made somewhat difficult given they each had children living with them. Tino had full custody of his eleven-year-old son. Pilar had joint custody of her two daughters, ages six and eight. After they had been dating about nine months, Pilar's ex-husband threatened to fight for full custody when the girls inadvertently revealed that Tino was spending the night at their house. After much discussion, Pilar and Tino decided to get married. Within a month they had married and were all living in Pilar's house.

Starting off "married with children" did not give the Gonzaleses the advantages of a nuclear family in which the couple has a period of time alone and the freedom to give all their attention to one another. In the stepfamily, your feet have to hit the floor running because there is this "instant family" with no history, no agreed upon rules, and everyone needing attention at the same time. It's common for the marriage to get short shrift, which is one of the reasons second marriages have a higher divorce rate than first. This is what happened to Tino and Pilar. The first year of their marriage was spent focusing on how their stepfamily was going to work. The children went to different schools, which required carpooling in two different directions. They were also very involved in after-school activities, so just getting through a week took a lot of energy and organization. The only break came when the girls went to their father's house two weekends a month. But even then Tino's son still required attention. As time passed, the marriage became less and less of a priority, running a distant third after work and children.

By the third year, Pilar and Tino were worn out and the marriage was in trouble. Stretched to the limit by the demands of a rigorous schedule and seemingly unable to make meaningful connection, they were existing in silent loneliness. Their sexual contact had become infrequent and perfunctory. They rarely went out alone for enjoyment, and affection for each other was sparse. Most evenings found Tino stretched out on the couch in front of the television and Pilar talking on the phone to her mother or girlfriends. They were more like roommates than husband and wife.

The Gonzaleses represent a common scenario with the neo-traditional family: two tired people with too much to do. Chemistry brought this couple together, commitment was keeping them together, but they were seriously lacking any form of compatibility. They had not stopped to ask the key question: "What is best for our relationship?" Like many couples, they thought making the kids the only priority was the best plan. But by ignoring the importance of their connection, they were cutting off the most powerful source of energy and rejuvenation. They were also not setting a good example of marriage for the children. They were ignoring an important fact: partnering is an important part of parenting. Many couples make this same mistake.

When the Gonzaleses came to me for help, it didn't take long for them to see their lifestyle was not reflecting their values, and their relationship was in a dangerously low spot. I asked them the key question: "What is best for your relationship?" In their own way they each answered "to get reconnected." Then I asked, "Is this also best for your family?" "Of course," was their reply. Then I said, "If you were to work as a team, starting right now, being creative and flexible, how might you address this situation?" I was amazed and moved by what they came up with.

After a few minutes of discussion and taking a closer look at the situation, then their options, they decided to invite Pilar's sister, who wanted to move to Austin, where Pilar and Tino were living, to come live in their garage apartment in exchange for carpooling the children to school and baby-sitting once a week. Tino agreed to ask his brother for a small loan to fix up the apartment for her. Realistically, they figured it would take about a month to put their plan into operation. Pilar agreed to call her sister; Tino agreed to call his brother. Just having a plan made them feel so much better that they left the session feeling more connected and relieved. I asked them to check back with me once their plan was in place.

Six weeks later I did hear from them and the changes were working extremely well. Tino's brother had not only loaned them the money for the remodeling but also helped with the work. Pilar's sister had moved in and was planning to enroll in the local community college next semester. They were doing well as a couple with the new freedom in their schedule, their once a week date night, and from the confidence they gained from turning a low time in their relationship into an opportunity to deepen their connection. By working as a team through this low spot, they discovered new strengths as a couple and reconnected as well.

Research has confirmed that most relationships die because of lack of connection. The Gonzaleses' lifestyle was not conducive to connection. They needed less stress and more time together to allow for kind gestures and acts of love to begin again between them. Tino and Pilar remind us that the low times indicate the need for a course correction, and that most often the correction concerns reconnecting.

IDENTIFYING DISCONNECTING BEHAVIORS

If you are feeling disconnected to your relationship, the first step toward reconnection is to ask: "What is best for the relationship?" The second step will likely be to discover how you are contributing to the disconnection. That is, to practice ownership by identifying your disconnecting behaviors. Look at the following list and check the ones you use.

overworking	being dishonest	being depressed	being perpetually late
criticizing	going silent	using sarcasm	being authoritative
interrupting	name calling	bossing	turning away
nagging	condemning	ignoring	controlling
withdrawing	forgetting	being rude	withholding affection
drinking	embarrassing	shaming	staying preoccupied
judging	lying	assuming	not supporting
being irritable	fault finding	coercing	interpreting
being distracted	being perfectionistic	being impatient	withholding sex
clinging	shutting down	being tense	expressing hostility
being resentful	overspending	being angry	being aggressive
threatening	lecturing	uncaring	showing suspicion
keeping secrets	being cynical	yelling	procrastinating
being rigid	avoiding	raging	always wanting more
name calling	lecturing	pushing	looking for problems

withholding your opinion

taking on too much responsibility

overfunctioning

being preoccupied with your own thoughts

being uncooperative

believing you have the right answer

being a pleaser

being undependable

other:_____

RECONNECTING

Once you take ownership of your disconnecting behaviors, the next step is to replace them. Think of the times you use these behaviors and make a plan of what you can do instead. The most effective way to reconnect is to take charge of your own actions. Don't worry about what your partner decides to do; you take the lead. It's in your best interest to improve your actions whether your spouse decides to do the same or not. You will feel better about yourself if you do the right thing. Claiming your partner won't cooperate is no excuse. It only takes one to stop the disconnecting. You be the one. Here are some suggestions how.

THOUGHT STOPPING

Thoughts affect feelings as well as behavior. If your heart is full of negativity, there will be no room for love. Even though pessimists are often correct, optimists are happier, live longer, and more fun in relationships. To illustrate why, think of a situation you detest. Focus on your disgust. While you are holding negative thoughts, pay attention to your body. Do you feel the tension or tightness in your gut, chest, or jaw? Look in the mirror at your expression. Imagine what that can do to your health over time—not to mention your relationships. Some of us have learned to look at the dark side of life. It's a way of preventing disappointment, but it has a harmful effect on our daily existence. If you have been in the habit of focusing on the negative aspects of your relationship and looking for faults in your partner, the simplest way to alleviate this situation is through thought stopping. Every time you are aware that your mind is going negative, just say STOP! You can say it out loud or to yourself. It's simple and it works.

TAKING RESPONSIBILITY FOR YOUR ACTIONS

Several years ago Vivian came to see me because she was anxious about attending her stepdaughter's wedding. Her husband's ex-wife and two stepchildren, who had been vocal about their dislike of her, were going to be there and she was not looking forward to it.

I helped her devise a plan by asking this question: "Vivian, how would you like people to see you at the wedding?"

She thought for a while and then said, "Well, I'd like other people to see me as happy, calm, and gracious."

"Can you recall a time when you felt this way?" I asked.

Vivian thought a couple seconds and then said, "Sure, last week at my sister's house."

"And how did you act?" I asked further.

"I talked to people, I smiled, laughed—just had a good time," she replied.

"Do you think you could intentionally carry that attitude into the wedding and make a conscious choice to maintain it?"

Vivian thought for a moment, then looked at me confidently, "Yes, I believe I can."

And she did.

Think about the kind of partner you want to be; then make a conscious choice to act in that manner. Refuse to let others control your behavior. Take responsibility for your own actions.

THE GATEWAY ACTIVITY

Given that love has natural highs and lows, it is important to have an activity that will always bring you back to a loving state. I call this the "gateway activity." For some couples sex is a gateway activity. It brings them back to closeness and contentment. For others, a quiet evening at home will do the trick. Simply saying "I love you" or "I'm sorry" can also be effective. Over time gateway activities may change; therefore, you have to exercise flexibility. The important point is that you always have at least one that works.

What have been the gateway activities that have worked for you in the past?

What gateway activities have you used recently that have worked?

Are there new gateway activities you'd like to try?

How often do you think you need to exercise these activities?

What are the warning signs that indicate that you are in need of reconnecting?

SEASONED SEX

Sex often plays a vital role in reconnecting couples, but there is not enough said or written about the importance of it in long-term relationships. Most of the hype is about new love, but the best life has to offer comes from true love. Public opinion is so slanted that we've been programmed to believe that deterioration of our sex life is endemic after the first two years of a relationship. However, this doesn't have to be the case, and it is not for millions of couples.

Lovemaking wanes when it takes a back seat. Time pressure from work, domestic responsibilities, commuting, and social commitments make it a challenge to find quiet, private moments with a partner. Nevertheless, if you are too busy for sex—maybe you are just too busy.

So what can we learn from the fortunate couples who use sex as a gateway activity and have managed to keep their sex life enticing through the years? Here are some tips.

Be generous with physical affection. Loving touch makes your partner feel good about him- or herself, promotes closeness between the two of you, and activates endorphins that cause you both to feel more calm as well as connected. Couples who stay sexually active and happy do not limit their expression of physical affection to the bedroom. Important truth: men are as hungry for affection as women are.

Be seductive in the basic ways. The old standbys are still important. Be thoughtful. Do special favors. Lavish loving attention. Be playful. Show enthusiasm. Look your best. One of my closest friends, Noelie, says you should go through your closet and give away anything that doesn't make you look drop-dead gorgeous. If nothing else, improve your posture, and smile. You can do that right this minute. Make sure your hygiene habits appeal to your partner. Lastly, learn to express your feelings during sex. It's feedback, it's erotic, it's instructional, and it's flattering.

Be sensitive to your partner's needs. The reason most couples don't have sex is that at least one person doesn't feel attended to. If you are a person with a high desire level, a high-T person, you may not need a lot of attention to be sexually aroused, but your partner, a low-T person, may. Be willing to meet your partner's arousal needs, and be romantic in the ways your partner prefers, even though it may not be your cup of tea. Bring flowers if they touch your partner's heart; fold the laundry if it makes him feel loved. Let your partner be your guide.

Be responsible for your own orgasm. This doesn't necessarily mean you do it yourself but rather that you take the initiative to know what arouses you and communicate this to your partner. Also, be aware that your partner may not always want an orgasm. For example, in their twenties and early thirties it is not uncommon for women to experience a surge of pleasure simply with penetration. This response is brought on by the release of oxytocin. When the vulva and vagina are stretched by the entry of the penis, it can give a surge of energy equal to the sensations of orgasm. Consequently, she may not feel the need to reach a climax. So, let her determine if she wants an orgasm. A man may also want to pleasure his mate without coming to orgasm himself. When each person is responsible for letting the partner know his/her needs, it takes the guesswork out of lovemaking, and avoids miscommunication and disconnection.

Make your lovemaking mutually satisfying. Many sexual positions favor the male orgasm and don't provide enough clitoral stimulation for the female. Few women can reach orgasm by intercourse alone. Most need manual or oral stimulation or a position for lovemaking that provides the necessary excitement. The woman-on-top position allows the female to stimulate her clitoris—either with her fingers or the movement of her body—while having intercourse. The man's hands are free for extra stimulation also. Rear-entry or doggie style intercourse allows for deeper penetration and is more likely to stimulate the G-spot, which is a highly erotic area in the vagina. In this position, the man has his hands free for caressing other areas such as the clitoris, breasts, buttocks, thighs, scrotum, and testicles.

If the woman sits on the edge of the bed, this position sometimes allows for interesting contact. Or, having sex while seated in your partner's lap can provide another variation. Having sex from the spoon position, with both partners lying on the right or left side with the man entering from behind, not only leaves four hands free but takes little energy and effort. Oral sex has come to be considered a staple of marital sex for many couples. As couples are remaining sexual long into later decades and require more stimulation, various forms of lovemaking have become more common and accepted. For men who may need more stimulation, oral sex can not only be pleasurable but also bring his penis to a greater state of erection for further lovemaking if that is what is desired. Though oral sex is a stretch for some individuals, you can work up to it gradually. Perhaps start with kissing different parts of each other's body—the stomach, inside of the thighs, and then later the pubic area.

Break the ice. Sometimes just trying anything new will get you out of a rut and open the door to further adventure. It doesn't have to be outrageous to simply interrupt your routine. It might mean having sex with your boots on or while you are coloring your hair. You have to start somewhere. Having sex with the lights on might ultimately lead to swinging from the chandelier. Finally: location, location, location. Just changing the location of where you have sex can add new excitement to your love life. Make it a point to have sex in every room in your home. Then move to the car, the back porch, the deck, behind the bushes in the backyard, your mother-in-law's bathroom. Then change the location of where you stimulate each other's body. Instead of confining kisses to the lips, go for the neck, thigh, shoulder, fingertips (for further instruction on fingertip kissing rent *Don Juan DeMarco* and watch the opening scene). Let your creative juices flow.

Expect and accept changes in yourself and your partner. The only predictable aspect of a sexual relationship is change; therefore, flexibility is important. As men and women go through the years together, hormones fluctuate, the body matures, and stress takes its toll. All affect your sex life. Satisfied couples accept these changes, manage them with care, and show mutual respect for one another's changing needs. Here are just a few of the changes you might expect.

Although familiarity doesn't have to breed contempt, eventually it will take the edge off the erotic tension. No matter how good your sex life is, over time you will need to vary it. Once your brain gets accustomed to a routine, it relaxes and you no longer have the benefit of the adrenaline high that comes with novelty and not quite knowing what to expect. In order to get your heart beating faster, you have to add an element of surprise and variation to keep the excitement.

Maturity brings its challenges, too. For example, as a man gets older he needs more time and stimulation to get aroused, and his erection may be less firm. His orgasm may also be less intense. It is important to understand that he may feel as excited as he ever did but his body does not respond the same, as quickly, or as spontaneously. The loving cooperation of a partner will more than offset these changes.

For women, perimenopause, which are the ten or so years prior to the cessation of menstruation, brings physical changes. Loss of sexual interest, vaginal dryness, and painful intercourse are all symptoms of this time of life. Again, without accurate information one can look to the relationship for causes that are purely physiological. Fortunately, there are many remedies for these symptoms such as Vagisil Intimate Moisturizer (VIM), a non-hormonal cream that keeps a woman moist and more receptive to sex. You can also alleviate symptoms by varying your lovemaking, and making sure you are fully aroused before penetration.

If you touch every day, address sexual problems before they become permanent, have some kind of sex regularly, treat one another with respect, share a romantic act, laugh, and play together, you will keep your sexual chemistry alive and stimulate all the cells that keep you living longer.

THE THREE CARDINAL SINS AGAINST CONNECTION

There are three common reasons why most couples aren't making a connection: 1) they don't spend enough time together; 2) they are not tuned in to one another; or 3) they are not intimate. Let's look at each of these.

TIME

It always strikes me as odd when I hear someone say, "I don't have time." I don't quite understand this statement because we all have the same amount of time: 24/7—twenty-four hours a day, seven days a week. What differs is how we choose to spend it. How you spend your time reflects your priorities.

There was a time (maybe it is still the case) when your relationship was given first priority in terms of time. Remember when you fell under Cupid's magic spell? You found time then. When infatuation called, you had time to answer. The fact is, most of us make time for our priorities and the activities we really enjoy. Spending time in a loving relationship is efficient because it gives you energy. You get back more than you give. In many cases couples have access to more time together than they use. It's just not rewarding enough to be an incentive, so maybe the most important question for you to ponder might be: "What would make me want to spend more time with my partner?" Or, "What would make my partner want to spend more time with me?"

Your Formula for Time

You are likely aware that in your relationship one of you is more of an extrovert and the other more of an introvert. Simply stated: an extrovert gets energy from being with people; an introvert gets energy from being alone. When the extrovert's energy gets low, he/she can call someone, go visit, or go to the mall to be with people and feel renewed. When the introvert gets tired, he/she is more likely to want to be alone, read a book, or take a walk. Although these two people are on opposite ends of the continuum, they each need time alone as well as with people, but their ideal formula for how they spend their time differs. Use the next exercise to determine your formula for spending time. There's a diagram for you as well as your partner.

The Time Formula

Think of the circle as representing 100 percent of the hours you spend awake in a given day—from the time you wake up to the time you go back to sleep. Divide your total waking hours into three sections that represent the amount of time you prefer.

1. Totally by yourself (alone time = A)
2. One-on-one with just the two of you (intimate time = I)
3. In a group of three or more (group time = G)

Example:

Jane—ideal formula   John—ideal formula

Now, you and your partner try it:

Partner No. 1   Partner No. 2
Ideal formula   Ideal formula

Take another circle, and think of your typical day (a workday would be best instead of a weekend or holiday). Chart the amount of time you ordinarily spend.

• Alone (A)

• One-on-one (I)

• In a group (G)

Example:

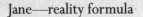

Jane—reality formula   John—reality formula

Now, the two of you chart the time each of you spends alone, together, or in a group:

Partner No. 1   Partner No. 2
Reality formula   Reality formula

Looking at Jane's ideal formula and comparing it to her reality formula, how do you think she might want to spend her time at the end of a workday?

Looking at John's ideal formula and comparing it to his reality formula, how do you think he might want to spend his time at the end of a workday?

How might this affect their connection? How could they work this out?

Now look at your ideal formula versus his/her reality. Is there a discrepancy? How might this affect your relationship?

Look at your partner's ideal formula versus his/her reality. Is there a discrepancy? How might this affect your relationship?

How might you use this information to your advantage and to strengthen your connection?

Too Busy for Love?

You have to spend a certain amount of time with one another to keep the connection strong in a relationship. Quality time occurs within quantity time. On the other hand, spending time away from each other can also add excitement and anticipation. The key is finding the right formula that works for the two of you. By making their relationship a priority, Pilar and Tino deepened their connection by renewing their commitment to each other, taking time to experience themselves working as a team in a compatible way, and renewing their energy through intimacy and sexual pleasure. They made an important course correction that deepened their connection.

TUNE IN

One of the most powerful ways couples connect is through being tuned in to one another. Truly pay attention, take an interest, and show that you care. My husband illustrated this beautifully. We were sitting in bed early one Saturday morning reading the newspaper and drinking coffee when he took the page he was reading and tore out a section and handed it to me.

"Here's the recipe for corn casserole from Fonda San Miguel's restaurant. Remember last year how you looked and looked for one?" At first I drew a blank, then I was incredulous. It had been so long since I had thought of corn casserole, but he was right. I had searched for that recipe for quite a long time last Thanksgiving. As I stared at the recipe, tears welled up in my eyes. I was so touched that he had remembered that little detail. I turned and gave him a big hug.

"This is one of the many reasons why I love you so much."

Listening, watching, remembering, and showing that you are

tuned in are simple ways to connect to your partner. I saw my son-in-law tune in to my daughter during labor in a way that deeply endeared him to me.

Devin walked every step with Kathleen as she paced the floor. When the pain became more intense, he held her as she tried new positions to ease the discomfort. He massaged her aching body as the hours wore on, and cried sympathetic tears with each contraction. Then when the birthing entered the last stage, he counted and panted with each and every push. When baby Katie finally made her appearance, it was evident to everyone in the room that it was through the efforts of both mom and dad. The picture that stands out in my mind of this sacred event is of Devin holding Kathleen and Katie as we all cried tears of joy.

Being empathetic and compassionate by trying to walk in your partner's shoes for a time is a powerful way of tuning in and strengthening your connection.

How well do you tune into your partner? How could you improve?

How well have you been paying attention to your partner?

See if you can answer the following questions:

What has been the high point of your partner's year?

What has been the low point?

What does he/she worry about most often?

If he/she could live anywhere in the world, where would that be?

What helps him/her manage stress?

Who is his/her hero? Heroine?

What is he/she most afraid of?

What has been the saddest event of his/her life?

What has been the most humbling event of his/her life?

What subject does he/she dislike talking about?

What activity does he/she enjoy most?

What does he/she get the most excited about these days?

THE "I" WORD

You rarely hear or read about relationships without the word intimacy coming up. But as much as you hear this word, I've had a lot of people ask me, "What is intimacy?" The best answer comes with a little poetic license.

> Intimacy = into me see.

When you are intimate, you let me see into your personal world through talking at a personal level or by letting me see a part of you not ordinarily seen by others. When I get a deeper understanding of your thoughts, feelings, ideas, and aspirations, then I can better relate to you. I see how we are alike, as well as how you are different. As I get to know you better, I can be more trusting and relax in your presence.

Many times in my work with couples I have seen barriers come tumbling down through intimacy. Couples who thought they were miles apart discover similarities through the sharing of personal thoughts. Couples with no hope find encouragement through revealing their deepest fears. Couples who believed their love was lost recaptured warm feelings as they told of their longings.

In most cases intimacy can only occur within the context of

safety. If you long for your partner to share with you—to reveal personal information with you—the key most likely will lie in your ability to create a safe environment. Can you do this? Specifically:

Can you listen without interruption?

Can you continue to hear when you disagree?

Can you be patient enough to hear it all?

Can you sit quietly as your partner explains his/her position?

Can you tolerate constructive criticism?

Can you be calm when your partner is not?

On the other hand:

Can you sometimes be the talker as well as the listener?

Can you give information in a nonjudgmental way?

Can you express yourself when you disagree with your partner?

Can you express yourself when you know your partner is not going to like what you say?

Can you be patient with yourself as you struggle for words to express what you are thinking and feeling?

Can you stand up for yourself and not let your partner interrupt or stop you from giving information?

Can you stand your ground when your partner is so much better with words?

Can you admit that it is difficult for you to talk—and then talk anyway?

When you are confused or going blank, are you able to say "Give me some time, I'm confused" or "I'm going blank"?

The Intimacy of Touch

Touching feels good, but that is only part of the story. As mentioned earlier, touching causes us to secrete endorphins, which not only protect us from pain but can make us glow with contentment.

Touch, which promotes physical as well as psychological intimacy, is a vital part of connection and plays an important role in the maintenance of closeness. Affectionate touching, either in private or public, is not only a physical gesture but also a message about the nature of the relationship. When you see two people holding hands or hugging, it's taken as a sign of closeness. Touch is often a barometer of the relationship. You can tell a lot about two people by the way they touch or avoid touching. The level of affectionate touch between partners can also be a measure of commitment.

Yet despite being told how important it is to have physical closeness, some of us grew up in an environment without much touching and are still learning to appreciate its merits as adults. The good news is that it can be done. Even if you grew up believing "I'm not a toucher," you can change.

Use the exercise that follows to help you assess not only your comfort with touching but also your personal preferences.

Touch Survey

Answer true (T) or false (F) to each question:

_____ 1. I enjoy most forms of touching.

_____ 2. I like it when my partner holds my hand in public.

_____ 3. I enjoy hugging my partner.

_____ 4. I get plenty of touching from my partner.

_____ 5. I am very affectionate toward my partner.

_____ 6. Touching is important to me.

_____ 7. I like to hug when we greet each other.

_____ 8. I am comfortable with a short, affectionate kiss in public.

_____ 9. I like falling asleep while touching my partner.

_____10. I am very clear about my partner's preferences for touching.

_____11. I like the role that touching plays in our relationship.

_____12. The way we touch keeps us connected.

There are no right or wrong answers to these questions. They are designed to be informative and raise your awareness about the role of touch in your relationship. Often we get preoccupied and just don't think about touching, and fail to take advantage of one of life's most healing experiences. The truth about touching is that it is good for you, physically, emotionally, psychologically, spiritually; and it's one of the most effective forms of connection.

The Intimacy of Kindness

Several research studies have shown that, generally speaking, happy stable couples treat each other kindly. Their conversations are respectful; their arguments don't escalate; they are nice to one another. If you and/or your partner wish to connect, this might be the next step for you. I am amazed at how many couples I have worked with that aren't even aware how rudely they treat each other. They don't realize how disconnecting and alienating it is to speak harshly, bark orders, correct one another, point fingers, lecture, and act in an unkind fashion. I am reminded of a couple I worked with in a workshop.

Grace and her husband, Roy, were a very attractive couple in their early seventies. At one point after I had been talking about communication, Grace called me over to ask a question. "What if your husband can't communicate?" she began. "My husband has had a stroke and he can no longer talk, so we *can't* communicate." As she said this I turned to her husband, who had the most sensitive blue eyes I had ever seen. I felt such compassion for him and couldn't help think how embarrassing this must be for him. Grace went on to talk as if Roy were not even there. I interrupted her gently, not wanting to embarrass her, but recognizing their disconnected state. I began by offering reassurance. "Oh, there are many ways to communicate. In fact, I can see, Roy, that you are a wonderful communicator." His eyes began to well up in tears when I said this. "And I imagine that since your stroke you are far more observant and sensitive and have learned to communicate through many other ways, just like you are communicating with me now." Then I went on to move them toward connection. "It's obvious how much you care for your wife, just by being here." As I said this Roy turned to Grace and let the tears flow. As Grace looked back at him I said, "Here is the man that adores you and I think you are feeling that. It looks to me like you are communicating really well." Grace nodded her head as she took Roy's hands and sat silently connecting.

Out of her own pain and loss, Grace was not aware of her unkind attitude toward her husband. She discounted him by speaking as if he were not present. She also underestimated him and blamed him for a lack of communication, when she was a big part of the cause.

Much of the unkindness that goes on between two people is subtle. It may involve speaking about the person when he is sitting there, or speaking for someone when she can speak for herself. It can even involve going on and on about a subject that the person is not involved in. Being respectful, kind, even gentle can go a long way toward connection. Check it out with your partner: ask if you treat him/her in a manner that promotes connection.

There are many ways of making connection. You can connect by making time for one another, by reassuring each other during the tough times, by celebrating, by meeting one another's needs through sex and affection, and simply by being kinder. What is important is that you and your partner decide which forms you will choose to satisfy each of you. Now let's take a look at friendship and how it relates to true love.

9

Connection: Forging a Friendship

I have the best set of friends a person could want. As I sit here writing, three of them are in Dallas doing their holiday shopping—and mine, too! Now, that's what I call true friendship. For the past six months, while the computer and I have been joined at the wrist, they have carried the responsibility of our friendship without complaint. They check in with me periodically, make sure I know about important events, give help however they can, and expect little or nothing in return.

Fortunately, they have been through this writing process with me before and know "this too shall pass." Soon I will be back to carrying my weight in the friendship. History says all the good times we have shared will be more than enough to get us through this long dry spell.

For a few moments, I'd like you to think about friendship and the role it plays in your life. Think of a person you would call a good friend—someone other than your partner—and see how many of the following statements apply to that relationship. Put a check mark beside the statement if it applies.

_____ 1. We support each other in the tough times.

_____ 2. We understand each other.

_____ 3. We enjoy one another's company.

_____ 4. We have a lot of laughs.

_____ 5. We treat each other with respect.

_____ 6. We enjoy a lot of the same things.

_____ 7. We trust each other.

_____ 8. We accept our differences.

_____ 9. We keep our relationship on a positive note.

_____10. We each put effort into our friendship.

_____11. We can depend on each other.

_____12. We settle our differences without threatening the relationship.

Now, go back over the checklist again, only this time, think about your relationship with your partner and see how many statements apply. What do your answers tell you?

Most satisfied couples will tell you that friendship is the most important ingredient in their relationship. What this means is:

- They have good times together.
- Their conversations are respectful.
- Their arguments don't escalate.
- They support each other.

Some couples build friendship naturally; others do not. The main reason why couples have difficulty being friends with each other is because they have never seen it done and haven't learned that it's important. Their image of marriage does not include the acceptance and support required in friendship, and they don't expect marriage to be fun or friendly.

Love ebbs and flows, depending on how you treat each other.

FRIENDSHIP DEEPENS LOVE

We like people who are nice to us, and if they keep it up we grow to love them. You can't expect someone to love you if you are rude, negative, despondent, critical, perfectionistic, dissatisfied, disrespectful, unsupportive, apathetic, and generally no fun to live with. Your partner might be dependent upon you, afraid of you, attached to you, even sexually attracted to you, but he/she will have a tough time loving you if you act this way most of the time. True love prefers a friendly environment, where each person is treated with respect. It can survive the highs and lows when it has lived in a rich soil long enough to develop roots and grow strong. In this day and age, when the average marriage doesn't last as long as a refrigerator, friendship is vital.

See how you fare in the friendship aspect of love.

True or False:

_____ 1. My partner would say I am as nice to him/her as I am to my best friend.

_____ 2. My partner feels very supported by me.

_____ 3. My partner sees me as a team player.

_____ 4. My partner will attest that my attitude is much more positive than negative.

_____ 5. My partner would say I am a fair fighter.

_____ 6. My partner would say I am fun to be with.

_____ 7. My partner loves my sense of humor.

_____ 8. My partner often sees me smile.

_____ 9. My partner would say that I am responsive to his/her needs.

_____ 10. My partner acknowledges that I have pulled us through some tough times.

_____ 11. My understanding nature keeps our relationship friendly.

_____ 12. I do my part in preventing harmful interactions between us.

_____13. I come up with fun ideas for us.

_____14. I initiate interesting conversations.

_____15. I'm a good sport.

_____16. I express optimism about our relationship.

_____17. I am known for my pleasant disposition at home.

_____18. I am accepting of imperfection in my partner and myself.

_____19. I have a realistic vision of relationships.

_____20. I am a pleasant person to live with.

Total true answers: _____

After answering these questions, do you think you are responsible for more of the highs or lows of love?

In a relationship where friendship is nurtured, each person takes personal responsibility for making the relationship better. It's not a 50-50 proposition. Each gives 100 percent. They may support the friendship differently, but both are mindful of its importance. It is the acts of kindness, sensitivity, and generosity that form a friendship.

Here are some examples of ways couples have deepened their love through friendship.

GETTING CREATIVE ABOUT MAKING TIME FOR ONE ANOTHER
Emilio and Sharon love to go out to dinner but with three young children rarely have time. Their dinners out are more likely to feature a Happy Meal than haute cuisine. But Emilio, determined that they would somehow make it work, came up with the idea that once a month he and Sharon would go out for breakfast. Once they get their children off to school, they head off to a fine restaurant and have a quiet meal together before going to work. An added bonus is that the topic of conversation always centers

on them as individuals or as a couple, and problems are never discussed.

LENDING A HELPING HAND

I collect a list of good marriages, those that I admire and look up to. Our closest friends, Nancy and Bill, have one that fits this category. One early Saturday morning, I went over to help Nancy with a garage sale she was having and there was Bill out hauling furniture, moving boxes, schlepping merchandise—all before the crack of dawn. Here is a guy who works long hours five days a week, plus being on call as a plastic surgeon. He has every reason to keep his hands—which are responsible for making his living—well protected. But there he was out helping Nancy before he went to the hospital to make rounds, and he isn't even a garage saler!

COMFORTING

When Todd's sister died, he experienced a grief he had never known. As children, he and Allee had been so close that it was hard for him to imagine life without her. Even six months after her death, he still found himself in deep mourning. Part of him was unable to believe that he would ever see her again. Because of his grief, he made the request to his partner, Haley, that they not celebrate his birthday coming up the following week. With complete understanding, Haley agreed that they would spend a quiet evening at home and forgo the usual celebration with friends; however, she did want to acknowledge his birthday, as well as his grief. With his mother's help, she came up with a loving solution. She collected an assortment of special photos of Todd and Allee throughout their lives, had them copied, then arranged them in a beautifully framed collage. She prepared his favorite meal at home, sent the two kids to the neighbor's, and had the house lit with candles when he arrived home from work. After they enjoyed their dinner, she handed him the present. He opened it with polite cheerfulness, but when he saw what it was, he didn't hold back his emotion. In the quiet of the setting, he let the tears flow as he looked longingly, with a kaleidoscope of memories, at each and every picture. It was one of the finest times these two married friends had shared with one another.

STAYING ABREAST OF EACH OTHER'S DREAMS AND GOALS

When Horace met Noelie, she was working at the cosmetic counter in Foley's department store. Being an astute businessman, it didn't take long for him to realize that she could be running the entire store herself. Noelie had grown up in a working-class family with parents who devoted their lives to making sure she and her sister, Jean, had everything they could give them. But a college education was not within their reach. Even though Noelie was very bright, she never recognized her intelligence. Instead, she relied on her beauty, wit, and charm to make her way through life. Horace saw beyond that. He recognized this diamond in the rough and for a wedding present gave her the promise of financing her college education. In return, she gave him four years on the dean's list and became the best financial manager money could buy.

CREATE A FRIENDLY CLIMATE

Years ago, I was working with a mother, father, and three children who had come to me for family therapy. They were having all kinds of problems "with the children," but it was clear to me that much of the stress in the family was coming from the husband's and wife's unfriendly attitude toward each other. At one point in the session, I got the idea to turn to the six-year-old daughter for input. "Sara Dell, what would you like to change about your family?" The four others first looked at me—surprised that I would consult the youngest member for advice—then they looked at Sara, who was ready with her answer.

"Well, it just hurts my feelings when everyone is yelling at our house." A tear spilled from her eye and ran past her little quivering chin as she spoke, then looked down at the floor. The room went silent with the truth of her statement. I just sat there and let the moment work its magic. That disclosure set about a chain of events that changed the climate in this family's home. They came up with the idea that every time someone yelled in an ugly manner, the adults had to pay $1, and the kids had to pay 10 cents. Believe it or not, it worked. Creating a friendlier climate—starting with the couple—changed the environment of the family and quickly brought therapy to a close.

HAVING FUN

One of the easiest ways to deepen a friendship is by having fun together. If you have a recalcitrant spouse, make an offer that can't be refused. Initiate an activity that you know he/she would enjoy. We like people with whom we laugh, and pleasure serves as a bonding agent. Fun is the gift that keeps on giving. We feel better and act better not only when we are having fun, but also for a significant time afterward. In order for this to work, the experience has to be fun for both of you. Make sure the activity you initiate is guaranteed to be thoroughly enjoyable. The list of options is endless in terms of activities that you and your partner could do for fun. To get an idea of what you each might enjoy, simply put a check mark by the activities you would be willing to take part in and you think would be fun to do together.

_____ playing cards

_____ dancing

_____ bowling

_____ going out to dinner

_____ going to a movie

_____ going to live sports

_____ skiing

_____ going shopping

_____ going out with friends

_____ planting a garden

_____ putting together jigsaw puzzles

_____ playing board games

_____ watching TV

_____ taking a drive in the country

_____ hiking

_____ going for a walk

_____ doing a hobby together

_____ planning a vacation

_____ rock climbing

_____ scuba diving

_____ snorkeling

_____ swimming

_____ taking dancing lessons

_____ learning another language

_____ entertaining

_____ cooking

_____ taking cooking lessons

_____ taking a wine tasting class

_____ playing video games

_____ going to an amusement park

_____ learning to fly an airplane

_____ flying a kite

_____ boating

_____ skating

_____ bicycling

_____ taking yoga lessons

_____ playing paintball

_____ playing laser games

_____ role-playing

_____ renting a video

_____ painting each other's body

_____ fishing

_____ hunting

_____ playing darts

_____ other: _____

_____ other: _____

Decide what you are going to do about bringing more fun into your relationship.

A JOINT PASSION

The optimal way to deepen friendship with your partner is through a joint passion. When I talk about finding your passion, people sometimes give me a blank stare and then ask, "How do you know what your passion is?" Because I have been asked this question so many times, I came up with a way for you to determine first your personal passion, and then a passion that you and your partner can share. Look at the following questions and think of one activity that fits each criterion. The activity that fits every statement will likely be a passion for you.

What one activity is it that:

- You look forward to with eager anticipation?

- When you are doing it, you lose track of time?

- Challenges you? Requires mental, as well as physical and emotional effort?

- While doing it you become entirely engrossed, absorbed, fascinated, and involved?

- Gives you energy even though it may cause mental or physical fatigue?

- When you are doing it, you have the overwhelming sense that this is exactly what you want to be doing?

Some of the answers people have given to this set of questions are:

skiing	gardening	sex	sailing	running
aerobics	reading	writing	singing	playing the guitar
dancing	painting	designing	woodwork	learning
traveling	rafting	bowling	fine dining	making crafts
hiking	camping	bicycling	cooking	watching a play
riding a motorcycle			playing with the children	
flower arranging			going to a concert	
going to the movies			rock climbing	
playing bridge			working crossword puzzles	
watching live sports			working around the house	

First, determine an individual passion that fits for you. Then, explore with your partner the activity that could be a joint passion for both of you.

It is important to the relationship that partners be supportive of each individual's passion as time and energy allow; however, one of the best ways for a couple to deepen their connection is through an activity they can enjoy together. Even if your relationship is at odds right now and you are feeling disconnected, chances are good that a joint passion is just what the doctor ordered. You don't have to wait until you are in a better place. Just do it. If nothing else, act *as if* you are having fun. You might be surprised how well this works. The truth about friendship is that it can get you out of the problems of marriage. If you've hit a dissatisfied lull, try spending some fun time together doing something you both enjoy. Ask yourself what you would do about the relationship if your partner were a friend in need. Be friendly, offer support, and try these words: "Honey, how can I be of help to you?" Then, be willing to step in and lend a hand.

Friendship begins at home, so let's move to a very practical side of love—living together—and how to create a haven for your love and relationship.

10

Connection: Creating a Haven

To be happy at home is the ultimate result of all ambition, the end to which every enterprise and labor tends.
　　　　　　　　　—Samuel Johnson, *The Rambler*, November 10, 1750

It's Friday evening about six o'clock when you walk into your home and shut the door on a long, hard week. Your body relaxes as the world outside fades into the distance and is replaced by the comfort of familiar sounds and smells. Looking around, you are pleased with what you see. Everything is just the way you like it. Taking a moment to breathe in the relief, you become acutely aware that "all is right in my world."

Does this sound familiar? When you walk in the door of your home, do you relax? Does it feel like a haven? Is it a place where your strength is renewed and your sense of balance restored? Is home where you and your partner serve as a source of comfort for one another, as well as a buffer to the outside world? Or is home a source of stress? Does another set of problems stand in the way of your satisfaction?

MAKE A HOME FOR BOTH OF YOU

Creating a home together is one of the significant steps in becoming a couple. Some complete this task easily; others never quite make it. When the decision is made to live in the same place, you are drawing a boundary around the two of you, separating you from the outside world and creating space for privacy and intimacy. Then, together you decide what the roles and rules will be inside your home.

Because a dwelling place is tangible, each person's participation is obvious. The dishes are done or they are not done. The bed is made or it's not made. There's little room for argument. You can't say, "I did make the bed. How did it get messed up again?" Or, "The dishes are done. I don't know what that is in the sink."

Since you can't dispute the facts, the inclination is to make it personal. E.g., "I didn't have time." "I'll do it later." "Okay, I'm not perfect!" You might be surprised to know how many couples have a problem coming to an agreement on how a home will look, feel, and operate. In essence, the home you create together will become a metaphor for your relationship.

UNDER CONSTRUCTION

Hayden and Lorey argued about the clutter. Hayden was handy around the house and loved to work on projects. The problem was, he had several going at the same time. Lorey felt like their house was always in a state of minor construction—a work in progress with no completion date. Hayden felt Lorey was unrealistic and that there were perfectly legitimate reasons for the uncompleted work. The new dishwasher was waiting for a part to arrive before he could finish installing it; the dining room had to be painted before he could put up the crown molding, and it had been raining too much for paint to dry. But in all honesty, this had been going on since day one. Neither Hayden nor Lorey were good at relating to one another. They were great workers and doers, but not so good at connecting. They were dedicated to work and to busyness, but not to their relationship. They had to learn to relax together, have fun together, and talk about mutually interesting subjects together before their home could become a haven for them and their relationship.

HOUSE BUT NOT A HOME

To say that Gaby took pride in their Victorian-style home would be an understatement. Despite the fact that she held a demanding position as the human resources manager in a large corporation, she managed to keep house like a full-time homemaker. She took pleasure in making her own draperies, upholstering furniture, and decorating the house. She was a dutiful mother, a delightful hostess, and compulsive cleaning woman. (Her husband, Barrett, said if he got up to go to the bathroom in the middle of the night, she would make the bed.) Even though he joked about it, her controlling attitude around the house was hard to live with. Somehow, she forgot there were other people living with her. She imposed her values and her standards on everyone else. Even though Barrett complacently went along, her oldest son and then her daughter rebelled. Finally, through the complaints and acting out behavior of the children, she and Barrett had to face their own issues. She saw how the house had been more important to her than their home, how she had been getting her domestic and creative needs met but was not attending to her intimacy needs, or to the needs of her husband.

HOME, SWEET HOME

If you ask Erin and Pierce what they need most in the world, they both will say "Sleep!" There never seems to be enough hours in the day to complete the tasks they lay out for themselves. Weekdays begin at 5:00 when Pierce gets out of bed. He is in and out of the bathroom by 5:20 so Erin can get in and out by 6:00. They wake up the three children at 6:15 in order to make the early school bus, which leaves at 7:00, enabling Erin and Pierce to get to work at 8:00. Some time during the morning drill, five lunches get made, breakfast is fixed, a load of laundry tossed in, the cat fed, daily schedules reviewed, and all the children get a quick inspection. Once the children leave at 7:00, Pierce and Erin have fifteen minutes to spend before they have to leave. They do their best to get in a personal conversation, tidy up the house a bit, and maybe fold a load of laundry. Whatever they leave undone will be waiting for them when they relieve the after-school baby-sitter about 6:00 in the evening. Then they do the morning routine in reverse. They eat as soon as possible, clean up the kitchen, help with homework, supervise play and bath time, and make sure the children get to sleep at a reasonable hour (somewhere between 9:00 and 10:00). Between 10:00 and 11:00 is what they call the "sacred hour," when they have an hour of quiet time together. Weekends they play catch-up, doing their best to support the children in sports activities, having some family time, running errands, and tidying up the house. They occasionally get a sitter so they can go out together. Time just does not allow for everything to get done. Both Erin and Pierce feel guilty that they are not doing enough. But if you ask them if their home is a haven, they would answer "You bet!" They love each other, are happy with their family, and thoroughly enjoy their home. Would it be featured in *Martha Stewart Living*? Maybe not, but their house probably looks a lot more like the typical family dwelling than the ones you see in magazines. The important point is the home works for them. They enjoy every inch of it, and Erin and Pierce figure they'll have many years in the empty nest to reorder their priorities.

Pierce and Erin are a good example of a couple who have come to a satisfying agreement about the physical condition and use of their home. They have learned what needs to be done to provide enough comfort and organization to make spending time at home pleasant and painless. As a result, they get a great deal of enjoyment and pleasure from the time they spend there. The house is not a source of conflict or difficulty; instead it is a haven for them and the children. They use it, take care of it as time allows, and do their best to keep it in working repair. They love their home, feel comfortable there, and feel safe from the outside world. Their priorities are comfort, efficiency, and user-friendliness. The house works for them, not vice versa.

MAKE HOME A HAVEN

Just a few decades ago, housekeeping had a standard set of rules most everyone followed. You washed clothes on Monday, ironed on Tuesday, then spent the rest of the week sweeping, dusting, cooking, doing dishes, and mending. Without the automatic washer and dryer, laundry took at least two, sometimes three days a week to complete. And without central heat and air, dusting and sweeping was needed several times a week to keep surfaces cleared of dirt and grime that entered through the open windows.

Modern technology has given us the luxury of choice. Now we don't have to wait for a sunny day to wash clothes and even the best housekeepers consider a weekly dusting acceptable. And furthermore, most homes do not have a full-time homemaker making the decisions about what is done when and how. The advantages of choice are obvious. No longer is one person a slave to housekeeping and arbitrarily assigned the household duties. Consequently, we have now thrown open for discussion all decisions about how to run the home and who will do it. But without teamwork and cooperation, the haven can turn into a haggle.

When there is discord in the living environment, it can affect all the hours you spend there. In order for a relationship to grow, it must have time set apart from the troubles of the world, as well as its own problems. The world of work comes with its own built-in difficulties (that's why we call it work) and maintaining a home has its challenges, too. But you have a lot more control over the way you manage your home than your work. If you and your partner can agree how to make your home a haven for both of you—as well as your family—then it can be a place of renewal where love can prosper.

THE ELEMENTS OF HOME

Think about what physical elements are important to you in a home environment. Then, look at the following list, ranking in order the top five descriptors in terms of importance, with 1 being the most important to you, 2 the next in importance, and so on, through 5.

_____ comfort		_____ neatness	
_____ charm		_____ relaxed atmosphere	

_____ beauty	_____ color
_____ cleanliness	_____ privacy
_____ efficiency	_____ having my own space
_____ open space	_____ quiet
_____ good lighting	_____ access to the outdoors
_____ personal touch	_____ character
_____ design	_____ easy to keep clean
_____ coziness	_____ convenient location of home
_____ user-friendliness	_____ decorating
_____ storage space	_____ close to nature
_____ other_____	_____ other_____

How would your priority list compare with your partner's?

What is one single thing that would make your home more of a haven for you?

What is the first step in making that happen?

IT'S A MATTER OF TASTE

Individuals differ in how they want their home to appear. Some like the designer look with everything put away and only objets d'art in full view. (I often wonder where all their "stuff" is.) Others take comfort in the coziness of clutter, feeling more relaxed when a place looks lived in. It's all a matter of taste. Use the following multiple choice questions to compare your taste with your partner's. Feel free to circle more than one answer to each question.

1. I would like our home to look like:

a) a feature in *Better Homes and Gardens* magazine

b) a place where real people live

c) it was just cleaned

d) a place you can put your feet on the coffee table, and that would be okay

e) other:_____

2. In terms of cleanliness:

a) I like the whole house clean and neat most of the time.

b) A little clutter makes me feel at home.

c) Neat is as good as clean.

d) Just so it's clean, I don't care if it is neat.

e) It's good enough for me the way we keep it now.

f) Other:_____

3. If I could change one thing about the way we manage our home it would be to:

a) hire (more) help

b) let more go

c) be more relaxed about it

d) divide the work more equally

e) other:_____

4. A good word for our decorating style is:

a) creative

b) contemporary

c) temporary

d) traditional

e) early marriage

f) other:_____

5. **If I were to grade our home in terms of it feeling like a haven and a source of comfort and support, I would give it:**

a) A

b) B

c) C

d) D

e) F

6. **The best way to sum up my feelings about where we live is:**

a) I'd like to move.

b) It's a drain on my energy.

c) I look forward to coming home.

d) Certain aspects of it bother me.

e) I'd like us to come to a better agreement about it.

f) Other:_____

7. **I think I could improve the atmosphere of our home if I:**

a) were neater

b) did more work around the house

c) relaxed more

d) learned how to do more things

e) got more involved

f) took more pride in how it looks

g) other:_____

8. **In terms of material items in our home, I think we need to:**

a) get rid of a lot

b) upgrade what we have

c) get some new items

d) replace worn-out pieces

e) check out the garage sales

f) have a garage sale

g) other:_____

How would you describe the atmosphere of your home? When you walk in, what is the first thing you notice? What thoughts come to mind? What do you feel? Is the environment conducive to the privacy and the solace needed to create a haven from the outside world?

STREAMLINE YOUR HOME

A few years ago, I became interested in feng shui, the Chinese art of placement. Last year, I bought myself a book entitled *Feng Shui for Your Home* by Sarah Shurety. The very first chapter was on clutter. Here's what it said: "The very first rule of feng shui is no clutter." I read that, shut the book, and went to work. In the next few days, my husband and I filled up his truck three times with clutter and took it to Goodwill. The house has been easier to manage ever since. That was about a year ago. I think it's time to do it again. According to laws of the universe, you have to make room for good things to come into your life. Start cleaning out, throwing away, recycling, donating, and loaning. Do whatever it takes to lighten your load. It'll make your life better.

I'm an avid garage saler, and fully half the items I buy are containers. I have bought every kind of container imaginable, from a nine-foot armoire to small decorative boxes. I find storing items out of sight—even if it's in a box under the kitchen sink—helps streamline the cleaning process. Our garage is full of storage units, shelves, baskets, file cabinets, hooks for the bicycles, big clips for the tools, and lots of marked boxes. I like to be able to put my finger on anything I need. It saves time and energy. (In terms of organization, the best single piece of advice I got years ago was: "Buy more underwear." Once I had enough for two or three weeks, it cut down my laundry time considerably.)

If these tips appeal to you, I recommend a delightful book, *Living a Beautiful Life: 500 Ways to Add Elegance, Order, Beauty and Joy to Every Day of Your Life,* by Alexandra Stoddard. This book makes me feel better just reading it. On the other hand, if both and your partner are happier in a cluttered home, then pile it on!

HOME IS WHERE THE HEART IS

This old adage implies there is more to a home than meets the eye, that home is a state of being, marked by safety, calm, happiness, and contentment. Home is the place where you belong, are accepted, understood, supported, and loved. Home is where people are interested in you. In her book *Home Comforts: The Art and Science of Keeping House*, Cheryl Mendelson, lawyer, professor, and homemaker, writes: "This sense of being at home is important to everyone's well-being. If you do not get enough of it, your happiness, resilience, energy, humor, and courage will decrease. Home is the one place in the world where you are safe from feeling put down or out, unentitled, or unwanted. Coming home is your major restorative in life." When I read this passage, I was struck by knowing that millions of people live in a home that is not a safe haven free from feeling put down, unentitled, or unwanted. I have heard too many accounts of criticism, belittling, harshness, anger, and blame to believe that every home is a haven. What I do believe is that having a home that serves as a haven is a major source of renewal, and it is vital to the pace we demand of ourselves in today's world.

So the operative questions are: Do you and your partner create a safe environment for one another? Are you truthful? Kind? Respectful? Loving? Is your home an emotional haven? Is your private time respected? Is your time together rejuvenating? Do you spend enough comfortable time there to be restored and renewed?

THE EMOTIONAL CLIMATE

Take a reading on the emotional climate in your home by placing a check mark on the line closest to the word that describes the atmosphere most of the time where you live.

Example:

Calm	. . . . ✓ . .	Agitated
Close	. . . . ✓	Distant
Cheerful	. . . .	Depressing
Quiet	. . . .	Noisy
Supportive	. . . .	Unsupportive
Tranquil	. . . .	Angry
Relaxed	. . . .	Tense
Accepting	. . . .	Unaccepting
Flexible	. . . .	Rigid
Pleasant	. . . .	Unpleasant
Friendly	. . . .	Unfriendly
Laid-back	. . . .	Rushed
Comfortable	. . . .	Uncomfortable

What is one thing you could do that could change the emotional climate of your home for the better? What do you need from your partner?

HAVEN HELP US

Imagine coming home from work and being greeted at the door with the aroma of your favorite spaghetti sauce simmering on the stove and the deliciousness of freshly baked bread in the air. Upon closer look, you see the table beautifully set with a fine table-cloth, china, silverware, and candles. Your partner is humming while putting the finishing touches on the salad, and you are welcomed to dinner with a hug and a kiss.

Or, try this scenario on for size:

You come home late from visiting a sick friend. The house is quiet, except for the strains of music coming from the bedroom. As you walk in, you smell fragrant candles burning and see the bed turned down with a rose on your pillow. You hear the sound of water running in the bathroom and look in to find a hot bubble bath waiting for you. You are not alone. Your partner is in the tub waiting for you, holding your favorite drink and wearing only a smile.

Or, finally, my personal favorite:

You have finally completed that big project at work and are looking forward to a long weekend at home. That is, until you remember what you have planned. This is the weekend you agreed to finally tackle that dirty house. It's been too many moons since you gave the place a thorough cleaning. The dust is so thick you could imitate the lunar landing, and you are sure the mold in your refrigerator holds the cure for something. Halfway between work and home you almost bolt. You think of any excuse to avoid going home. But deciding you are a grown-up, you straighten your shoulders, take a deep breath, and head in that direction. The first sign that something is different comes when you don't have to step over the old newspapers that had been collecting outside the front door. But that is just the beginning. When you walk in, you cannot believe your eyes. Your partner jumps up and says "Surprise!" You look around and there are the housekeepers finishing up the cleaning. Everything is sparkling clean and your weekend still awaits you.

You can create your own scenario if none of these appeals to you. The point is: it is delightful when someone makes home a haven, although you do not have to go to these extremes every day or week. But when someone goes to the effort of making home more pleasant, comfortable, or welcoming, our lives are more satisfying. The problem is, we all want it but sometimes forget that it works both ways. One person can't always be on the receiving end—or on the giving end. Partners have to create a haven for one another, whether it is physical or emotional. Everyone wants to come home to a delightful setting, tailored to meet his or her needs; however, how do you make that happen?

Look at the following questions and determine how much you agree or disagree with each one. This list will help you determine where you might begin to create a haven for both you and your partner.

DOMESTIC AGREEMENTS

Read each sentence and circle the number that best describes your answer.

1. My attitude sometimes makes our home uncomfortable.

Disagree   Somewhat Agree   Agree

   1   2   3   4   5   6

2. Right now, our home is in need of some serious attention.

Disagree   Somewhat Agree   Agree

   1   2   3   4   5   6

3. It's difficult for me to completely relax at home.

Disagree   Somewhat Agree   Agree

   1   2   3   4   5   6

4. Our home looks better than it feels.

Disagree   Somewhat Agree   Agree

   1   2   3   4   5   6

5. Our busy work schedules negatively affect the atmosphere of our home.

<u>Disagree</u>   <u>Somewhat Agree</u>   <u>Agree</u>

1   2   3   4   5   6

6. More often than not, I am totally exhausted when I get home after work.

<u>Disagree</u>   <u>Somewhat Agree</u>   <u>Agree</u>

1   2   3   4   5   6

7. Our home does not reflect my taste.

<u>Disagree</u>   <u>Somewhat Agree</u>   <u>Agree</u>

1   2   3   4   5   6

8. Our home does not meet my needs.

<u>Disagree</u>   <u>Somewhat Agree</u>   <u>Agree</u>

1   2   3   4   5   6

9. When it comes to keeping up with our home, I feel like I am always behind.

<u>Disagree</u>   <u>Somewhat Agree</u>   <u>Agree</u>

1   2   3   4   5   6

10. What our home looks like is not of great concern to me.

<u>Disagree</u>   <u>Somewhat Agree</u>   <u>Agree</u>

1   2   3   4   5   6

11. The biggest problem with our home is not being there enough.

<u>Disagree</u>   <u>Somewhat Agree</u>   <u>Agree</u>

1   2   3   4   5   6

12. I think our home is just fine the way it is.

    <u>Disagree</u>   <u>Somewhat Agree</u>   <u>Agree</u>

    1   2   3   4   5   6

13. I always feel good when I walk into our home.

    <u>Disagree</u>   <u>Somewhat Agree</u>   <u>Agree</u>

    1   2   3   4   5   6

14. I feel appreciated at home.

    <u>Disagree</u>   <u>Somewhat Agree</u>   <u>Agree</u>

    1   2   3   4   5   6

15. I feel safe in our home.

    <u>Disagree</u>   <u>Somewhat Agree</u>   <u>Agree</u>

    1   2   3   4   5   6

16. I like the location of our home.

    <u>Disagree</u>   <u>Somewhat Agree</u>   <u>Agree</u>

    1   2   3   4   5   6

17. I think our home is very welcoming to others.

    <u>Disagree</u>   <u>Somewhat Agree</u>   <u>Agree</u>

    1   2   3   4   5   6

18. Our home is private enough for me.

    <u>Disagree</u>   <u>Somewhat Agree</u>   <u>Agree</u>

    1   2   3   4   5   6

19. I feel respected at home.

    <u>Disagree</u>   <u>Somewhat Agree</u>   <u>Agree</u>

    1   2   3   4   5   6

20. I think my expectations of our home are realistic.

<u>Disagree</u>		<u>Somewhat Agree</u>			<u>Agree</u>
1	2	3	4	5	6

Scoring: Generally, these questions are best used for discussion or reflection. Your scores do not measure anything specific. However, depending upon how you interpreted the question, a high score on questions 1 to 10 might indicate that your home is not a haven for you; a high score on questions 11 to 20 might indicate that your home is a haven for you.

THE SILENT ENEMY

Without a doubt, the biggest challenge a couple faces when attempting to create a haven is lack of time. A home becomes a haven when your heart is there, but your body has to show up, too. Your connection to home is in direct correlation to your physical and emotional investment. The alienation you feel when not connected to home can easily be confused with alienation from your partner.

Countless times I have seen couples mistake work burnout for partner burnout. When you are worn out, overworked, and run-down, your judgment can be affected. It is also impossible to give from a burned-out state. One person can carry a relationship for a period of time, but not forever. Couples often take the relationship for granted and don't structure their lives to include the necessary time to recharge themselves and their partnership. We all need downtime without work, chores, hassles, or responsibilities. And we need sufficient time at home and with the people who live there to maintain a satisfying relationship.

WHATEVER HAPPENED TO SUNDAY?

Some years ago, when my son, Jimmy, was in the army, he and his wife, Colleen, were stationed in Germany and I went to visit them. Even though he worked on base, they chose to make their home in a German village in order to get to know the local people and to take full advantage of the culture. On the first full day of my visit, Jimmy was briefing me about the German way of life. "There are a lot of things different here, Mom. First of all, on Sunday, everyone is quiet. You don't mow your lawn or wash your car, and you don't play loud music. Everyone stays around the house or takes a walk."

I still remember the impact of his words. I had to ask myself, "Whatever happened to Sunday in the U.S.?" I could remember when Sunday was truly the day of rest. Sunday was the time some people went to church—but everyone rested. They sat on the porch, or played with the children, took a nap, or visited the sick. Sunday was also the day that families got together over a pot roast or fried chicken. But more than that, Sunday was the day that balanced the rest of your week. It was set apart from the other six. No one expected you to work, call in, or check your messages. Most stores were closed. It was a day of restoration, renewal, and contact. Some people believe the earth was created in six days. Why do we think we need all seven to do far, far less?

Work expands to fill the time you have to complete it. If you want time at home, it will only happen at your hands. Here are some tips:

Make your priorities and stick to them. Decide what it would take for you and your partner to feel connected to your home in a satisfying way. Then, build an iron fence around those priorities! Expect the transition time to be tough and fraught with many temptations. But once you start reaping the benefits of this investment in home improvement, it won't be so difficult.

Develop rituals that protect your time at home. Many couples have a date night or family night that becomes sacred. Some families make sure to share at least one meal a day together. Others have religious rituals that organize time. Make sure that each week has a ritual that brings you together at home. Whatever the means, schedule your time to include what is most important to you and let the world know these rituals are an important part of your life.

Maximize your time together. Make the time you are home together count in the ways that mean the most to each of you. Do chores together. Catch up on reading while sitting in the same room. Take a shower together. Wash each other's hair. Run errands together. Go to bed at the same time. Get up ten minutes earlier to have a cup of tea together. Make sure you greet each other properly and keep each other informed. Honor one another's alone time. Run interference for each other to protect that time. Take turns handling tough tasks. Make sure you have fun together, but above all, make the time together satisfying for both of you.

Take advantage of modern technology. That is: turn off the TV and turn on the answering machine. Take time to be together in the quiet of your home. Develop the art of interesting conversation. Learn to ask open-ended questions that encourage conversation. For example: "What went on at work today?" "How did the meeting go today?" "What did the children have to say after school?" "Where would you like to go on vacation?" "What would you do if you knew you couldn't fail?" "If you could have any job, what would it be?" "What is your opinion about_____?" "How do you feel about_____?" "What are your thoughts about_____?"

The truth is, it takes more than a house to make a home. Creating a haven will provide a safe place and a retreat from the outside world, which is necessary if you want to nurture one another and let your relationship develop roots and grow. But you also need support from the outside world. We'll look closely at this issue in the next chapter.

11

Connection: Providing Support

SUPPORT IS LOVE IN ACTION

Support is a vital part of true love. If you are among the fortunate who have a supportive partner, you live with the assurance that no matter how tough life gets you never have to face it
alone. You know that at the end of a long day, the comfort you
need awaits you. Not only is your home a haven, but also within
your partner lies a source of strength available to you. Whatever
you endeavor—whatever you strive for—is made easier and far
more possible through the ongoing energy provided you by the
support of your relationship.

I doubt anyone would disagree that we live in very stressful
times. Given this fact, there is even more need for a relationship
to be a source of comfort and support. We all need someone in
our corner who, when push comes to shove, will be there for us.
We need someone who will call "Foul!" when life throws us a
curveball; who knows when to come close and when to honor
distance; when to speak and when to listen; when to embrace and
when to stand by silently; when to make suggestions and when to
wait for the request.

Providing support is one of the most efficient ways of creating
and maintaining a satisfying relationship. When individuals feel
supported by their partner, the relationship has far less conflict and
far more goodwill. Dedication grows deeper and love grows
stronger. The best news of all is that support is easy to give because
most stress comes from outside the relationship. This offers a
chance for couples to join forces as they provide comfort in a world

that can be less than comfortable. It is much easier to fight the forces outside the relationship than to deal with conflict between the two of you. However, the key to support is knowing the difference between when you are the problem and when you are the solution, that is, being able to distinguish relationship problems from outside stresses. This e-mail sent to me by a friend illustrates this:

A man and woman have been in a relationship for about four months. One Friday night, they meet at a bar after work. They have a few drinks, then go to get some food at a local restaurant. They eat, then go back to his house and she stays over.

Her story:

"He was in an odd mood when I got to the bar. I thought it might have been because I was a bit late, but he didn't say anything much about it. The conversation was quite slow-going, so I thought we should go off somewhere more intimate so we could talk more privately. We went to this restaurant and he's STILL acting a bit funny and I'm trying to cheer him up and start to wonder whether it's me, or something else. I ask him, and he says no. But you know I'm not really sure. So anyway, in the cab back to his house, I say 'I love you' and he just puts his arm around me. I don't know what the hell this means because, you know, he doesn't say it back or anything. We finally get back to his place and I'm wondering if he's going to dump me! So, I try to ask him about it, but he just switches on the TV. Reluctantly, I say I'm going to go to sleep. Then, after about ten minutes, he joins me and we have sex. But he still seemed really distracted, so afterward, I just wanted to leave. I dunno, I just don't know what he thinks anymore. I mean, do you think he's met someone else???"

His story:

"Shitty day at work, low on funds, tired. Got laid, though."

When I read this, I laughed out loud. I could see myself doing the same thing the woman did. There have been many times I have taken my partner's attitude personally when it had nothing to do with me. One morning, I noticed that my husband, Spanky, was being more quiet and a little distant (my interpretation, of course). I immediately personalized his behavior and began reviewing our interactions the night before.

When I couldn't come up with anything I had done, I tried my least invasive inquiry: "How are you doing, hon?"

"Just fine," he replied as he went about his morning routine.

I didn't get any insight until about mid-morning, when he walked into my office and said, "I just got off the phone with the vet. He thinks Blue [our wirehaired fox terrier] has meningitis. He's going to call in a new prescription and I'm going to go pick it up."

At that moment, I understood what the silence had been about. Blue had been critically ill for over two months. Despite every test and treatment our veterinarian could suggest, Blue's lethargic condition had not improved. His immune system had failed, he could barely walk, and was sleeping 99 percent of the time. He had such trouble breathing, many times we thought he was taking his last breath. After weeks with no improvement, the night before we had raised the option of taking him off the massive doses of medicine and letting him die in peace. We had had this conversation before, but with every little sign of hope, we'd avoided taking that step. When the vet called with the new diagnosis of meningitis, we had hope again. Spanky cheered up and his despondency lifted. I realized that I had not been the problem—and could clearly be part of the solution.

WHY WE TAKE IT SO PERSONALLY

The field of psychoneuroimmunology has given us a scientific explanation of why, at times, we take our partner's attitude personally. The reason is, we impact each other. Humans do not live in their own private sphere. We breathe the same air, feel the effects of the same force of gravity, and rotate on the earth at the same speed. We also take in energy and send out energy just like we inhale oxygen and exhale carbon dioxide. All human processes interact with the environment and other humans are a part of that space; therefore, we impact one another.

We know, for example, that two people standing about four or five feet apart will have a physiological effect on one another. One person's heartbeat will be registering in the other's brain wave pattern, and vice versa. Two females living together will unconsciously, over a course of a few weeks, synchronize their menstrual periods. A man living with a woman will have an elevation in his testosterone level around the time she ovulates. Two people lying side by side will start to synchronize their heartbeat. New information is showing us that in some very important ways it is impossible not to take it personally when your partner is upset or preoccupied because you will feel it at some level.

When this happens, it's not a bad idea to check to see if you have been living up to the agreements between the two of you. If you have not, then take immediate steps to get back on course. This periodic self-examination will keep you accountable and aware of your actions. If you are not a part of the problem, then make sure you are part of the solution. Years ago, when my husband went silent, instead of making a simple inquiry like "How are you doing, hon?" I might have pried, grilled, or forced him to talk about something before he was ready. He has often said to me, "You think out loud, so you are always ready to talk, but I have to mull it over in my own head for a while before I'm ready to talk about it." I have learned to give him space and time to work his own process. The biggest challenge in doing this was learning to manage my own anxiety. In the past, I might have gotten so anxious with his silence that even an argument would be preferable to feeling shut out. Over time, I've learned that being patient feels supportive to him and is good for me.

Despite the fact that most stress is not caused by the relationship, stresses can affect the relationship. Many couples come together at night exhausted from dealing with a broad range of responsibilities throughout the day. There are issues related to children, aging parents, conflict with neighbors, health concerns, financial strain, crime, traffic—and we haven't even mentioned work.

Today, jobs are more demanding than ever, requiring longer hours, greater energy, more responsibility, and offering less security. Work stress can come from deadlines, personality conflicts, intense competition, miscommunication, technological glitches, an unrealistic job description, downsizing, reorganization, relocations, poor management, lack of cooperation from co-workers— the issues go on and on. Now, with a growing list of overnight millionaires, even people in their twenties feel like they should be doing more. Salaries are higher than they were ten years ago, but the toll work takes on your life is higher, too.

A couple years ago, when my son finished his MBA at Harvard, he traveled about the country being courted by corporations. The offers he received were mind-boggling. Six-figure salaries, sign-on bonuses, stock options, moving allowance, and money to pay off student loans were common in the packages. But as one CEO put it, "We see ourselves as the next Microsoft and our motto is 'Lead, follow, or get out of the way.' You will be well compensated for your work here; however, an eighty-hour week is not uncommon. If this sounds like too much, then this job isn't for you."

To his credit, Jimmy didn't take that or any job that had these requirements. He was fortunate to have options; however, that is not always the case.

Sometimes life throws us a challenge—like the death of a colleague, an ailing friend, an unfriendly job market, or additional work hours—and we have no option but to cope with it. Ideally, during these times your relationship is a big part of your coping mechanism, serving as a source of comfort, a sounding board, and a buffer from the outside world. When under stress, most of us are not at our best. At these times, it is vital to have a partner who is sensitive and understanding enough to recognize the distress signals and come to our aid in ways that are most helpful. It would be ideal to say that we should be able and willing to ask for help, but the reality is that when most of us are under stress, we are least likely to seek help. When you're busy fighting alligators, it's easy to forget you have friends on the shore. Over time, having a supportive partner who comes to your aid will teach you that help is available, and it's okay to ask.

THE BEST OF TIMES, THE WORST OF TIMES

Each life challenge provides you and your partner with an opportunity to deepen your love and dedication. Look at your best friends. They are the ones who have been with you through thick and thin. They understood your depression when your mother died. They held your hand when your heart was broken, and commiserated with you when you didn't get that promotion. People bond through supporting one another during the tough times. This is a key element of dedicated love.

Brandi had always wanted to be a hair stylist and when her aunt died and left her some money, she and her husband, Mick, agreed that this would be a good time for her to pursue her dream. With the inheritance, they had just enough funds to offset the loss of her salary while she went to school full-time. During the first year, her hours were flexible enough for her to get the children off to school in the morning and be there when they got home in the afternoon, so it all worked out well. But during the last six months of her training, she had to attend classes in the morning and then style hair in the afternoon and most evenings Monday through Friday. To help out during this time, Mick asked his mother to come over after school to be with the children until he got home. She agreed to do this. After the first couple weeks, however, the schedule began to wear on Brandi. She missed the time with her family and the long hours were exhausting. By the time she got home in the evening, the children were already in bed, so she got up early to spend time with them before they went to school. She was so tired, though, her disposition was anything but pleasant. Most mornings found her in an argument with either one of the kids or Mick before they left the house. When she got home on the Friday evening after her third week, Mick asked her to sit down and talk with him while they ate the pizza he had ordered.

"The kids and I have been talking, and we'd like to propose a plan. We all miss spending time with you, but we know this is only for about five more months. So, until you finish your training, we're suggesting that on Tuesdays and Thursdays the kids stay up until you get home so you can spend time with them, and then you sleep in the next morning. On Mondays, you are fresh from the weekend, so those mornings go well. Tuesdays, you can sleep in because you will be able to see the kids that night. Wednesdays, you can get up if you feel like it, but you sleep in on Thursdays because you will see them that night. This will give us time together and give you a chance to catch a little more sleep. What do you think of that?"

"I think I have the best family in the world."

When one person in the relationship is under stress, it affects the entire system. Whether stress makes or breaks you as a couple depends upon how you manage it. If you see it as an opportunity to show support and help one another, it can deepen your love and dedication.

Many of the stresses in life come from outside forces. The extent to which a couple can create a supportive environment to offset and help one another manage those stresses is a clear predictor of their ability to create true love.

The truth about love is that not nearly enough attention has been given to the effect the external environment has on it, not to mention the nature and function of a relationship. Far too often we look at the relationship as the cause of stress, not the victim or antidote to stress. Professionals, too, have been guilty of this oversight. Counseling and therapy more often focus on problems rather than how the individuals support one another. Far more research has been geared toward couples' conflicts than on how they support each other. Yet relationship happiness is more strongly correlated with support than resolving problems. This lack of attention to social support in marriage may be a significant oversight in our understanding of the development of marital distress, as well as marital success. Relationships do not exist in a vacuum. Each individual interacts with the outside world in various ways. To fully understand your partner, as well as your marriage, you need to look at the big picture. Take into account all the issues they deal with, and not just with each other. So many times, a couple comes in to see me and says something like, "Our relationship was fine until about three years ago."

Then I ask the obvious: "What happened three years ago?"

The answer is something like, "Well, we went through bankruptcy, but that's not what caused our problems."

As we begin to look at how the stress from that event showed up in their relationship—and how they supported one another during this time—we discover they did not use this life challenge as an opportunity to work as a team. Instead, they let it divide them.

The newest research has not only shown us that relationship satisfaction is directly related to how partners support one another, but that a lack of support leads to dissatisfaction and conflict. Couples, as well as professionals, tend to focus on the conflict. Unfortunately, they are going after the symptom, not the cause. This is so sad because it is far easier to learn support skills than to learn conflict resolution. Going back to my earlier example, once Spanky came in my office and told me about the vet's call, I understood what his silence had been about, and it was easy for me to provide support. As soon as he told me, I got up from my chair, went over and hugged him. I didn't have to say anything; I just held him and we shared a few tears. It was easy to console him because he wasn't upset with me. When I am the source of his discomfort, it's much more natural to defend myself than show support.

Developing support skills will not only lower your stress, but also greatly reduce conflict. Under stress, we are vulnerable and sensitive to rejection. A negative response during this time can be devastating to the relationship and ignite the fires of conflict. On the other hand, a supportive response can go a long way toward strengthening your dedication and creating satisfaction. Learning how to support your partner is one of the simplest and most effective ways of improving your relationship. With support, you are more likely to be optimistic, to spend time together, be open to new experiences, and to fulfill one another's expectations. Let's take a quick look at what both you and your partner need to feel supported. What you will likely find is that the two of you sometimes need the same type of support and other times a different type of support. It is important to know when to give what.

A SENSE OF SUPPORT

Complete the following sentences to help you learn support skills:

"When I've had a hard day, what helps me is . . ."

"When I am worried about something, it helps if . . ."

"When I am totally stressed out, I need to . . ."

"When I've been alone for a long time, what I need is . . ."

"When the job pressure gets to me, what helps is . . ."

How does your partner need to be supported?

Do you feel confident in knowing how to support your partner?

What questions might you ask your partner about support?

What additional information would you like your partner to have concerning his/her support of you?

DISTRESS SIGNALS

Research indicates that individuals who are able to ask their partner for emotional support when in distress are far happier than those who do not. But in order to ask for help, you must have enough self-awareness to know when you are in distress. A sensitive partner will often know before you do. Ideally you both will come to recognize your own distress signals, as well as each other's. Most relationship conflicts begin with one person under duress from sources outside the relationship. The sooner one of you can recognize the distress signals and provide or ask for support, the more likely you will avoid conflict and resolve the issue by working together in a constructive way.

One of the many advantages of being married or in a committed relationship is having someone to talk to and to help you deal with the inevitable highs and lows of life. For this reason, support and friendship are cited as the two most common reasons given for marriage. A large part of relationship satisfaction is working as a team to combat what the world sends you each day. Consequently, one of the final tasks in creating true love is to recognize the distress signals used by you and your partner so as to expedite the support process. Let's begin by having you discuss some basic questions concerning distress.

DETECTING DISTRESS

Answer the following questions. If you are not completely clear, ask your partner.

How do I act when I am stressed?

How does my partner know when I am starting to get stressed?

When stress is at its worst, what am I like?

How do I act when I am worried?

How do I act when I am trying to figure out a solution to a problem?

How do I act when I am frustrated?

Tips:

- Do whatever it takes to become familiar with the early warning signs of stress for you and your partner.

- Develop effective ways of supporting one another during times of stress.

- When you know your partner is stressed, this is not a good time to bring up issues about the relationship. This is one reason why living with ongoing stress is so bad for relationships, because there is never a good time to bring up these critical issues.

- It is important to develop the skills that enable you to know when you are the problem, and when you are the solution.

- Advice is usually not helpful unless your partner directly asks for it. Unsolicited advice can be experienced as dismissive and condescending.

- If your reaction to your partner's problem is greater than his/her reaction, then you may be taking the focus off of him/her and putting it on yourself. This isn't supportive in the long run.

- Practical suggestions can be helpful after support is given and your partner is open to hearing them.

- Emotional support and commiseration are helpful to some people, but others see it as discounting their ability to handle the situation.

- It is important to realize that silence can scream louder than anger. By saying nothing, you can actually be communicating a hurtful message.

- Even though your anger or rage may not be intended for your partner, he/she still feels the fallout.

- We all need to recognize that it is unrealistic—and perhaps detrimental—to expect our partners to always be there to support us every time we are in distress. Sometimes, a family member, friend, or an expert may be the more appropriate choice.

- It takes a village to have a relationship. On a regular basis, couples need contact with friends, relatives, and others who believe in and support their relationship.

- Giving consistent attention to the importance of support in your relationship will prevent many conflicts.

- A supportive environment fosters love, trust, happiness, and commitment.

THE TRANSITION RITUAL

One way to leave the stresses from the outside world outside is to come up with a ritual you use at the end of each workday that divides work time from home time. Some people use their drive home as a transition ritual; others sit down and watch the news to shift gears. What is the ritual you use? If you don't have one, what are some ideas? How can your partner be more supportive of this transition time? How can you support your partner with his/her transition time?

SHOW SUPPORT

There are many ways to show support. Use this list to generate ideas for both you and your partner. Rate each example in terms of how helpful this form of support would be when you are worried or stressed.

Not Helpful		Helpful		Very Helpful	
1	2	3	4	5	6

1. Ask me "Is there anything I can do to help?"

Not Helpful		Helpful		Very Helpful	
1	2	3	4	5	6

2. Point out that I seem stressed.

Not Helpful		Helpful		Very Helpful	
1	2	3	4	5	6

3. Give me space and time to work it out myself.

Not Helpful		Helpful		Very Helpful	
1	2	3	4	5	6

4. Listen to me.

Not Helpful		Helpful		Very Helpful	
1	2	3	4	5	6

5. Ask if I want to talk about it.

Not Helpful		Helpful		Very Helpful	
1	2	3	4	5	6

6. Have sex with me.

Not Helpful		Helpful		Very Helpful	
1	2	3	4	5	6

7. Give me advice.

Not Helpful		Helpful		Very Helpful	
1	2	3	4	5	6

8. Ask me questions about what is going on.

Not Helpful		Helpful		Very Helpful	
1	2	3	4	5	6

9. Pitch in and help out with what needs to be done.

Not Helpful		Helpful		Very Helpful	
1	2	3	4	5	6

10. Take over some of my responsibilities.

Not Helpful		Helpful		Very Helpful	
1	2	3	4	5	6

11. Give me physical affection.

    Not Helpful   Helpful   Very Helpful

    1   2   3   4   5   6

12. Take me out for some fun.

    Not Helpful   Helpful   Very Helpful

    1   2   3   4   5   6

13. Give me peace and quiet.

    Not Helpful   Helpful   Very Helpful

    1   2   3   4   5   6

14. Spend time with me.

    Not Helpful   Helpful   Very Helpful

    1   2   3   4   5   6

15. Tell me you are interested in what is going on with me.

    Not Helpful   Helpful   Very Helpful

    1   2   3   4   5   6

16. Tell me you love me.

    Not Helpful   Helpful   Very Helpful

    1   2   3   4   5   6

17. Tell me some good news.

    Not Helpful   Helpful   Very Helpful

    1   2   3   4   5   6

18. Do your best to cheer me up.

    Not Helpful   Helpful   Very Helpful

    1   2   3   4   5   6

19. Cook my favorite meal.

   Not Helpful   Helpful   Very Helpful

      1   2   3   4   5   6

20. Suggest we go for a walk.

   Not Helpful   Helpful   Very Helpful

      1   2   3   4   5   6

These questions are merely for insight and discussion. Look at your ratings and think about your responses, or talk about them with your partner.

HIGH/LOW

In the movie *The Story of Us,* the parents and their two children had a ritual of asking each other at the end of each day, "What was your high today?" and "What was your low?" In this manner, everyone got a short time to debrief each day's stresses and celebrate the victories. It was also a good way of keeping everyone informed about each other. Try it this evening. Each of you tells the other what the high point of your day was, and what the low point was.

If this ritual doesn't appeal to you, think of another way that you can empty the trash on your mental computer. You might use "Here's what I liked about today" and "Here's what I didn't like about today."

Another idea is to rate your day on a scale from 1 to 10. Tell why you chose that number. Example: "Today was an 8. If the weather had been warmer, it would have been a 10. I nearly froze going from the car to the store, but I got a lot done and I feel relieved."

GETTING IN THE HABIT

It's time to fish or cut bait. You've been reading about support, now is the time to ask for it. Think of a specific issue that you can address with your partner that has nothing to do with the relationship. Here are some sample ways of bringing these issues up:

"One issue I could use some support with now is. . . ."

"You could help me by. . . ."

"What I specifically need is. . . ."

"If you did that, I would feel. . . ."

GETTING IT RIGHT

If you and your partner can learn to recognize distress signals and provide support in effective ways, you will be making an investment in true love. Mutual support is a greater predictor of relationship satisfaction than resolving conflict, having a great sex life, or even having money. The skills are not difficult to learn. The key is to continue to educate one another in the art of loving. You are now acquainted with the truth about love. For some of you, this completes your journey; for others, it just begins. To bring this study to a close, let's move to the concluding and final chapter, "Claiming Love."

12

Claiming Love

The truth about love is that it is available to everyone, and all you have to do is recognize it, and have the courage to accept it.

After a keynote speech I gave recently, a woman named Jackie came up to me and said, "I'd really like to find true love, but I keep being attracted to the wrong guys."

Since I'd heard this comment hundreds of times before, I knew to ask, "Are you attracted to the ones who are not available?"

She gave me a startled look, and as her face flushed answered, "Yes, the ones that are never interested in me."

I continued kindly, "I'm wondering if it feels familiar to have someone not interested in you, and when you meet a guy who is interested, you don't feel anything for him?" Jackie nodded, fighting back tears. "Then perhaps you have to learn to tell the difference between turmoil and true love. Tumultuous love is what we see in the movies. You may be familiar with the excitement of turmoil, but unfamiliar with having someone who loves and cares for you. So when a loving, available guy shows up, you feel bored or uninterested. My advice is to slow down, pay attention to the nice guys, and let yourself be loved. You deserve it. Love is out there, you just have to learn to recognize it."

The tears fell as Jackie nodded in agreement and gave me a warm hug. I asked her to e-mail me and let me know how her story continues.

This brief exchange reminded me how easy it is to love someone who is unavailable, or to believe that a better partner is "somewhere out there." This way you never have to face the fact that you have difficulty loving and being loved. As long as you believe no one is available for you, you can avoid looking at yourself and facing the truth that you may be more familiar with longing than loving. I know Jackie can find love. The more important question is, can she accept it?

CLAIM THE LOVE YOU DESERVE

As I complete this book, the final truth I want to leave with you is this: love is all around you and all you have to do is claim it. The best way to begin is to see love in your partner's behavior; in the thoughtful gestures you take for granted; in the everyday kindnesses shown to you. Focus on what your partner gives you instead of what you are not getting. I know that as simple as this is, it is also difficult. I spent years ignoring the love around me. I encourage you to claim the love that is there for you, and remember:

Love is available to everyone. To experience true love you need the courage to see it, believe it, and let it in.

"The course of true love never did run smooth." Shakespeare was right; love has highs and lows. The high times give us those loving feelings and the low times alert us to the need for a course correction.

Love has normal, predictable stages. Infatuation brings you together. Post-rapture gives you a taste of reality. Discovery provides the way out of inevitable low spots. And connection brings you full circle to a deeper experience of love. You cycle through these stages time and again, each time coming closer to the heart of true love.

You keep love alive by acting in a loving way. Love doesn't last; you have to *make* it last. True love replenishes itself daily through acts of kindness.

Love must have form and function. Love is made manifest in deeds. The role you play in one another's life as well as the way you express your love determines the course of true love.

Love is what matters. When all is said and done, love is what we remember. On your deathbed you won't say "I wish I'd made more money, I wish I had worked more." You will grieve the lost opportunities for love, and celebrate the ones you had.

Love reaches its highest form in commitment. When two people decide to make their love exclusive and permanent, they take fear out of the low times and give energy to the high times. They also set forth on a spiritual path.

Marriage is the partner of true love. Commitment is good for you. Men and women alike are far more likely to achieve their personal goals when accompanied through life by a faithful partner.

I hope this book has encouraged you on the path to marriage as well as true love, for ultimate commitment is the gateway to love. Only by closing the door behind you, do you open all the possibilities love has to offer.

Love enhances life and takes everyone in its path to a higher plane. With true love you accomplish more, live better, and come far closer to reaching your potential. I wish you well on your journey. Here are some final guidelines:

- Celebrate the highs.
- Learn from the lows.
- Keep discovering one another.
- Keep your mind open to the possibilities of love.
- Be open to change.
- Be kind.
- Be clear about the roles you are following.
- Be trustworthy.
- Make your relationship a priority.
- Find out what says "I love you" to your partner, and do it.

- Deepen and protect your connection.
- Form a friendship with your partner.
- Make your home and relationship a haven.
- Foster mutual support.
- Look for love in your life every single day.

A FINAL STORY OF TRUE LOVE

When Edna and Curtis married in 1943, he had to borrow two dollars for the license because they wanted to get married on Valentine's Day, and he didn't get paid until the end of the month. They didn't have a honeymoon; but Edna said living with Curtis was all the honeymoon she ever needed. Throughout their life, no matter how many disappointments they faced, she always managed to have a positive attitude.

At the time they married, Curtis was working as a clerk in a grocery store, and the owner let them move into a small apartment upstairs. Edna began keeping the books for the owner part-time. Within their first year of marriage, she was pregnant and about the time Tommy was born, Curtis became the manager of the store. With his promotion, they were able to move into a house and plan a second child. Edna got pregnant right away. Six months into the pregnancy she developed toxemia, and had to be put on complete bedrest. Her condition became serious and the doctor feared for her life as well as the baby's. Curtis lost twenty pounds in three months, just worrying about his family. When Jenny was born she weighed a little over five pounds and had little strength. But Edna nursed her to health and in a short time the family was doing well again.

As the years rolled by, their marriage prospered. Edna continued to work part-time from home, helping out with the accounting for the store in the evenings. Curtis took care of the children while she worked. (They had a neo-traditional family before it was fashionable.)

By the time both children were in grade school, Edna and Curtis had saved enough money to buy the grocery store, and she worked there during the hours the children were in school. Throughout the years, their family worked as a team. They supported one another through financial hardships, the death of family members, health problems, even a break-in at the store. Through it all their love supported them and continued to grow deeper.

Tommy and Jenny both graduated from college, married, and between them produced five grandchildren. And, even though the siblings and cousins could fight like cats and dogs, when they were in Edna and Curtis's home, they lived in peaceful coexistence.

The years rolled by, as did life, and by the time Edna and Curtis reached their early eighties, their family had expanded to include three great-grandchildren. Their home continued to be a gathering place for holidays and family occasions even though the grandchildren had spread across the country. Two weeks after his eighty-eighth birthday, after a particularly hard winter, Curtis was taken to the hospital with pneumonia. It came on him suddenly, and he got very ill in a short period of time. As fate would have it, while he was hospitalized, Edna went into cardiac arrest and was placed in the intensive care unit of the same hospital. All the children and grandchildren were called to the hospital. Although Curtis was very ill, it was apparent that Edna had even less time to live. The doctors were able to keep her out of pain, but her heart was growing weaker. The last evening she was alive, Jenny called her brother, Tommy, to Edna's bedside and said, "I can't bear the thought that Mother and Daddy will never be together again before she dies."

"What can we do?" asked Tommy.

"We can move one of them," replied Jenny.

They looked at one another knowingly; then, without words, went to work.

They walked to Curtis's room, put his oxygen tank on the dolly Jenny had gotten from the supply room, and wheeled him bed and all down the hall and onto the elevator. When an orderly saw them coming off the elevator, Tommy waved him away and they quickly moved their father's bed into Edna's room. They put Curtis's bed right next to their mother, lowered the rail, and helped him roll into her bed. In an instant, he surrounded her with his arms and the children left them alone. When they returned Edna was sleeping restfully and Curtis was stroking her hair and face. He kissed her goodbye one last time and the children helped him back into his bed. He didn't take his eyes off her until they rolled him out the door, leaving her to drift into eternity. Curtis never made it home from the hospital. He recovered from the pneumonia, but not from the loss of his one true love. But true love never dies. I know the love of this union still lives today in the lives of their children, grandchildren, and great-grandchildren. I have seen it with my own eyes in the life of the youngest grandchild, who is a friend of mine and one of the most loving men I have ever met.

My wish for you at the close of this book is that you will have the delight of infatuation, the challenge of post-rapture, the excitement of discovery, and the blessings of connection. Love waits for you patiently. It waits for you to have the courage to take the most exciting journey of your life, one that has incredible rewards and unlimited opportunity.

Acknowledgments

First, I would like to pay tribute to two very special people, Helen Lakelly Hunt and Harville Hendrix, whose friendship and support have been invaluable to me over the past twenty years. It was through their work in the best-selling book *Getting the Love You Want* and Imago Relationship Therapy that I began learning about the true nature of relationships. For the inspiration of their personal and professional lives, I am forever grateful.

In addition, I would like to acknowledge my colleagues at the Institute for Imago Relationship Therapy, including master trainers Joyce Buckner, Bruce Crapuchettes, Maya Kollman, and executive director Rick Brown. To them, I say thank you for challenging and supporting me all these years. And a special recognition to my Imago buddy and master trainer, Sunny Shulkin, whose clinical wisdom is the finest I've ever seen and whose savvy is sprinkled throughout this book.

Also, to my colleague Jon Carlson—who never sleeps—my heartfelt gratitude for inviting me to be a part of the *Living Love* video series and for the privilege of working with so many experts from the field of relationship education. The days I spent with John Gray, Harville Hendrix, Michele Weiner-Davis, William and Carleen Glasser, Gay and Kathlyn Hendricks, Richard Stuart, and Jon were an invaluable contribution to this book.

I wish to further acknowledge the untiring dedication of Diane Sollee, director of the Coalition for Marriage, Family, and Couples Education, whose contribution to the field of marriage education stands out to me as a prime example of one person truly making a difference. Diane's belief in my work inspired me to put all that I have learned from her and the outstanding faculty of the coalition into this book.

And to my editor, Kris Puopolo, I owe a debt of gratitude for the expertise that made this book a product I'm proud of. I also say thanks to Kris for being a delight to work with and a breath of fresh air. Her excitement for this book supported me through many episodes of doubt and despair. I say thank you once again to my mentor and friend Ed Jacobs. Thank you for teaching me most of what I learned in graduate school and sending me forth into this magnificent profession.

And to my husband, Michael (Spanky) Stephens, who kept me in an endless stream of coffee, Cokes, and snacks, I am forever grateful, not just for the creature comforts but for the wondrous gift of simply bearing witness to what it takes to write a book. I couldn't have done it without you.

To all the people who have shared their lives with me, I pray that this book pays adequate homage to your stories. Thank you for giving me the gift of trust and the privilege of intimacy.

And finally to you, dear reader, I say thank you for making this work possible. My best to you in learning the truth about love.

Index

About the Author

Pat Love, Ed.D., is a marriage and family therapist and relationship consultant. She cofounded the Austin Family Institute and was its executive director for many years. In addition to her private practice, she lectures, gives workshops, trains professionals, and appears as a conference and keynote speaker. She is the author of two books, *Hot Monogamy* and *The Emotional Incest Syndrome*. She has been a guest on many national and local television and radio programs, including *Oprah* and the *Today* show, and has contributed to many popular magazines. She is a master trainer in Imago Relationship Therapy, a past president of the International Association for Marriage and Family Counselors, and a founding member of the National Academy of Marriage and Family Counselors.